...ops roy
u noble roy
ore comme
ie et derrai
inne de ces
lt espouse
du beau.
son vinant
ounes du

Christian
Stories of
Wisdom

Translation copyright © 2016 Black Dog & Leventhal Publishers

All rights reserved. In accordance with the U.S. Copyright Act of 1976, the scanning, uploading, and electronic sharing of any part of this book without the permission of the publisher constitute unlawful piracy and theft of the author's intellectual property. If you would like to use material from the book (other than for review purposes), prior written permission must be obtained by contacting the publisher at permissions@hbgusa.com. Thank you for your support of the author's rights.

First published in France under the title *Contes des sages chrétiens* by Nathalie Leone © 2005, Éditions du Seuil

Black Dog & Leventhal Publishers
Hachette Book Group
1290 Avenue of the Americas
New York, NY 10104
www.blackdogandleventhal.com

Printed in China

IM

First Edition: February 2016
10 9 8 7 6 5 4 3 2 1

Black Dog & Leventhal Publishers is an imprint of Hachette Books, a division of Hachette Book Group.

The Black Dog & Leventhal Publishers name and logo are trademarks of Hachette Book Group, Inc.

The Hachette Speakers Bureau provides a wide range of authors for speaking events. To find out more, go to www.HachetteSpeakersBureau.com or call (866) 376-6591.

The publisher is not responsible for websites (or their content) that are not owned by the publisher.

Library of Congress Cataloging-in-Publication Data available upon request.

ISBN: 978-0-3163-0929-5

Christian Stories of Wisdom

NATHALIE LEONE

Collection directed by
Henri Gougaud

Translated by Elizabeth Freeman

BLACK DOG
& LEVENTHAL
PUBLISHERS
NEW YORK

Introduction

This book has not been written to be read,
but to be consulted as a close and secret
    friend.
You can ask it
for nourishment, and it will feed you,
for enlightenment, and it will enlighten you,
to move you, to play with you, and with you
    it will play
in the most mysterious way the game of
    chance
that does not exist.

You may ask it a question full of hope
or anxiety, and at all events, an intimate
one—one of those questions which are out
of the reach of intelligence and which are
usually asked with one's heart, with closed
eyes. Open the book at random and it will
be there to speak to you. It does not only say
something more or less interesting—no. It
also answers the question that you have not
even uttered aloud. It responds in its own
fashion, which is perhaps disconcerting.
But do not wince. What you are told always
turns out to be surprisingly sensible.

It is a game that has been played for cen-
turies with books, which need to be constantly

loved to remain alive and to continue to be effective, despite the accumulation of time. Before unfurling their banners, innumerable princes consulted the Bible in this way, or the Koran, or the Vedas. Many spiritual wayfarers, or people who are momentarily lost, or alone, or just anxious to avoid an obstacle—in short, you and I—have thus asked these fairy tales for light to fill their beacon lamps. And these tales have thereby given them the light they needed.

Why, how, and from where do the answers spring? You should not explain that. Neither should you speak too much of them. I know from lifelong experience that tales are immemorial and benevolent older people. They know the music of the world's pulse. They always answer our questions, as long as these are asked with the innocence by which they themselves are shaped.

Keep this book close to you. Open it from time to time, as one visits a friend. And should you need advice from a luminary soul on your innermost path, consult it just by way of a game. Close your eyes. Open the book. Open your eyes. Thank whomever you wish.

Henri Gougaud

Pſin
ſachi
ſe poi
nea g

les guerres de fran
deugleterre eſtcomme
premierement Je le vi
et racompteray en br
Verite eſt que le bon ro

Contents

Introduction 8

Bernard and Francis 15

A Conscientious Monk 21

The Desert and the Locust 22

The Louse 25

Prayers Heard! 31

Providence 32

The Knight and the Keg 35

Three Pieces of Advice from a Bird 45

The Miser 49

The Clothes Chest 56

Saint Francis and the Wolf 57

Pope Gregory 65

The Hermit's Cat 68

Lying 70

The Monk's Three Sins 71

The Misdeed 74

What Jesus Said About the Clean
    and Unclean 76

Laundry 77

Saint Peter Beaten Twice 80

Abbot John Recounted This ... 83

Saint Peter's Mother 86

The Tale of the Fellow Masons 91

The Call   95
The Workaholic   97
Recreation   101
Saint Vincent   103
Saint Peter's Lie   106
The Foundry Worker   107
Temptation   119
Agatha's Absence   121
The Wind   126
The Virgin's Mill   128
Tadik-Coz   133
Entry into the Kingdom   138
The Parable of the Ten Virgins   141
Death   143
The Wood Chippings   145
The Epileptic Possessed of the Devil   151
Strange Miracle!   153
The Mantle of Christ   156
The Angel and the Hermit   159
Attention   163
Saint Bruno   165
No Lawyer in Paradise   167
Saint Yves and the Sailor   171
The Eloquent Preacher   177

The Bad Judge	179
The Lettuce	181
Advice	182
The Visit to Father Poemen	185
The Devil's Castle	187
Saint Peter and the Goose Keeper	191
Thoughts Focused on God and on a Beautiful Woman	195
The Priest's Cow	197
Christ's Debts	199
Saint Martin and the Two Rascals	201
The Fall	205
Straw	205
Peace	206
Rendering unto Caesar	207
The Quarrel	209
One of You Is the Messiah	211
The Good Thief	215
The Ray of Sunlight	218
The Lost Sheep	223
The Holy Grail	225
Sign of the Father	233
The Monk and the Bird	234
Photography Credits	237

Bernard and Francis

Francis had just withdrawn from the world and had embraced complete poverty. But the people of Assisi, his friends, his parents, and his acquaintances of long standing all thought him mad. They held him in contempt. When he went into town, people jostled him, threw nuts at him, and scolded him. They insulted him to his face and hurled at him all abuse they could think of.

Francis bore everything, without getting angry. He never even answered them.

Now a man was observing him from the window of his house. He was surprised to see him put up with such scorn so readily. "Either he really is completely mad," he said to himself, "or he has received special grace from God."

This man's name was Bernard of Assisi, and he was one of the noblest and richest citizens in the town. He sent for Francis, inviting him to spend the night in his home. He had a comfortable room prepared for him and in the same room had a bed set up for himself behind a drape. He wanted to watch this man of God and see whether he gave in to the comfort. He placed a large lamp on a chest of drawers, with sufficient oil in it to shine throughout the night. By evening the humblest of men and the richest man in the town slept in the same room. But rather than enjoying the fresh sheets and soft mattress, Francis soon got up again and prayed through the night. Like a litany, as if to spur his soul to be fruitful, he repeated: "My God and Everything, my God and my Everything; may God be Everything. May God be Everything." By the first glimmer of daybreak, Francis appeared to be illuminated too, and Bernard was deeply moved. Thanks to the lamp, which was still lit, but above all thanks to Francis's glowing devotion, nothing in the scene had escaped him. The rich man wished to be similarly ablaze with such passion.

"Brother Francis, let me take leave of the world and follow you," Bernard begged.

"I don't know . . . ," replied Francis, "you will have to consult Our Lord. . . . It is a serious decision. . . . You are powerful and accustomed to being honored."

But he looked steadily into the rich man's eyes and added these words:

"Follow me. Let's go see the priest at the bishop's palace. After the service we will pray until terce. Then we will ask him to open his missal three times in succession. And according to the words to emerge from the book, we will know what to do."

They listened to the service, and prayed until terce; the priest approached them and, at their request, opened his missal three times.

On the first occasion the book said:

"If you wish to attain perfection, sell everything you possess and give the proceeds to the poor."

On the second occasion they read:

"Let he who comes after me give himself up, take up his cross, and follow me."

On the third occasion the sentence ran:

"Do not take anything with you along the road."

Brother Francis turned to Bernard of Assisi and said, "God has given you his advice; . . . now it is up to you to prepare."

Bernard hurried home, settled his affairs, and sold all his possessions that same day.

In the evening he joined Francis in the poor district of the town, dragging behind him a big chest that contained his entire fortune.

They halted in a small piazza. There they took off their robes and filled the piazza with the many coins from the chest. A few onlookers drew near. These were the first to benefit, for the two men were scattering the golden coins around them as a peasant sows his seeds. Bystanders ran to and fro, their steps unpredictable, their eyes wild, and their hands grasping greedily. Jubilation spread throughout the town.

Once the chest was empty, Francis and Bernard left Assisi and set off on their journey.

A Conscientious Monk

A monk, having at a very young age entered the monastery where he spent twenty years, had misgivings as to his progress. He decided to visit Father Joseph, who welcomed him warmly and listened to him.

"Father," began the monk, "I am trying to follow the rules. I fast, I observe the contemplative silence, I carry out the work in monastery, I pray, I endeavor to banish vain thoughts ... What more can I do?"

The old man stood up, looked at the sky, raised his arms, and, stretching out his fingers that resembled rays, said to him, "Why don't you turn yourself into a flame completely?"

The Desert and
the Locust

A young monk who had just reached the desert decided to consult an elder.

"Father, I have been living here for one year and locusts have come six or seven times already. You know what a scourge they are. They infiltrate everything, enter the tents, slip between the blankets, make their way into clothing. They even hop into food ... I am at my wit's end."

The elder, who had been living in the desert for forty years, answered him:

"The first time a locust fell in my soup I threw away the lot. On the second occasion

I threw out the locust and kept the soup. The third time I ate everything—soup and locust. Now when a locust attempts to get out of my soup, I put it back in."

The Louse

In a monastery in the Loire region, there lived twelve monks under the lax law of their father abbot. Lulled by the rhythm of the seasons, working in the fields, transcribing manuscripts, and fulfilling duties, they were quite happy and had no other desires.

But one day the father abbot died. After respecting the mourning period, the twelve monks gathered one morning in the common hall, where they looked at one another in dismay.

Having entered the monastery at almost the same time, they were like true brothers. So who amongst them was going to take the place of father abbot?

"Brother Jacques."

"No," Brother Jacques moaned in response. "I ... I ... would never be able to. I ... I ... stammer."

"What about you, Brother François?"

"If you don't mind, I feel more at ease where I am ... "

"That leaves you, Brother Anthony."

"Which Brother Anthony? The very thought of it! I can't even remember my name. Why not Brother Denis?"

"Knowing my bad luck, the monastery would be struck by lightning before the end of the month."

"So who then?" bemoaned Brother Mathew.

"Why not you?"

"Me? I can never remember anything. How do you expect me to recite prayers by heart?"

And one by one each monk shrunk from responsibility.

The meeting lasted a long time. One by one the monks, depleted of their strength, slumped down in their chairs. Never had they spent so much time in conversation ...

Suddenly, one monk who had fallen asleep sat up:

"I've got it. God has just whispered the answer to me."

"So who?" asked Brother Mathew.

"I don't know."

"Do you or don't you know?" asked Brother Anthony, somewhat agitated.

"I'll be back."

Brother François left the room. He gave a sigh of pleasure, for the meeting had tired him out and he felt extremely stiff. He stretched himself and greeted the warm shining sun. He walked along the passageway as far as the porch and left the monastery.

He went down the little pebble path and reached the wood. Below in a glade a young shepherd was sitting in the shade while watching his flock grazing. The monk approached him and asked: "Could you give me . . . ?"

"I possess nothing," replied the shepherd bluntly.

"I only want a louse. You won't be any the worse off with one less louse."

"Why do you want a louse?"

"We are short of lice."

Without understanding, the young shepherd rummaged in his matted hair, and from amongst the microscopic mites that occupied his beard, chose quite a big louse.

The monk, overjoyed, took it gingerly between his fingers and went back to the monastery.

"Look, my brothers," he said as he went through the door of the great hall. "I have a louse here. Place your beards on the table and I shall put the louse in the middle. The louse will choose the beard, and the beard will indicate the father abbot."

Some of the monks were a little shocked. Two or three flicked their beards over their shoulders. But since most of them found the idea an excellent one, their beards were already spread on the big wooden table. Brother François, with his hand in the air, holding aloft the louse, waited for everyone to comply.

Eleven beards were laid out on the table, side by side. With a solemn gesture

Brother François placed the louse in the middle of the table and hastened to spread out his own beard at the place left for him, his chin on the table.

The louse set about smoothing out its back, under the noses of the monks who were examining and eyeing it. Then slowly it stood on its legs, scratched its belly, and began to notice the beards on display. For a louse this sight was the land of milk and honey. It inspected grey hair; jet black, bushy, disheveled, and dull hair; glossy and shiny hair; long beards, as well as those that scarcely showed below the chin; the greasy and the unremarkable. Finally it settled on the three hoary bristles of brother Jacques, the stutterer. The louse clung with love for a long-term visit.

The monks stood up respectfully and broke into a Benedictine chant.

So Brother Jacques, acting under coercion, became the abbot, elected by the louse.

At the beginning he stammered a little, but in the end he spoke quite clearly. Some said this was the effect of the louse that had taken up lodgings in his beard. No one knew exactly how this miracle was wrought. Let us say that thanks to the Almighty, the louse enabled the man to reach the heights of his calling.

Prayers Heard!

Two men in conversation were seated on the edge of a public fountain whose fine jet of water splashed them gently.

The first man said:

"When I need a favor, either for myself or others, I ask for it on my knees, behaving with the good Lord as I would with a merchant who seeks only to dispense his surplus knowledge. And I pray, ask, and beg."

"Are your prayers always answered?" asked the other man, skeptical.

"Always. Either the favor is granted or I feel my will merge in such a manner with God's will that, at that very moment, I wish for everything he wishes for."

Providence

A priest had shut himself in his cell to write a sermon on divine providence.

Suddenly he heard an explosion. The dam that protected the small town had just given way and the river burst its banks in a roar of flood water that swept along everything in its path.

The priest, distraught, was about to give way to panic when he caught sight of his sermon on divine providence. He pulled himself together and calmed down.

The village was flooded and most people stayed cloistered indoors. Some of them, however, did venture out, waist-deep in water, in search of help. A rescue boat soon arrived under the presbytery windows.

The rowers called out to the priest, gesticulating to him.

"No, no," he said to them, "this is the moment to believe in divine providence. I am staying where I am, without attempting to flee, and I shall pray. God will save me."

The water rose and reached the level of his window. He noticed a small boat making its way to him from a considerable distance. The rescuers could barely keep on course on the turbulent river, but they managed to get through. They shouted, "We have come to fetch you." And they reached out their hands to him.

"No, no," said the priest. "I trust that God will save me."

But the water continued to flood everything in the valley. The priest had to climb upward, and he soon found himself on the roof of the church.

Other boats were launched to save the remaining survivors. When these rescuers caught sight of the churchman perched on the steeple, they called out to him:

"Hurry, Father! Get in!"

"No," replied the priest. "I thank you, but divine providence is infinite. God will save me."

So the boat moved away. The level of the water continued to rise. Soon the man had nothing left to cling to.

For a while he tried to keep his head above water, but his strength wore away. He disappeared under the waves, and drowned.

Hardly was he dead than he arrived in paradise. He was beside himself. Furious. Without waiting to be announced, he barged his way in to see the Almighty.

"I preach divine providence, my Lord; I believe in you with all my soul, and what happened . . . Nothing!"

"What do you mean, nothing? I sent you three boats and you wouldn't get into any of them!"

The Knight
and the Keg

The knight was as comely as an angel. Even if he rode all day, on his return he was fresh and the folds in his clothing were as unruffled as they had been before he set out.

And yet he spread horror. He desecrated, burned, killed, and ravaged men and beasts who crossed his path. He was so cruel that people even thought he was born heartless.

He did not distinguish between respected holy days and normal days, never went to church, and never fasted, not even during Lent. And rumor had it that he had never in his life heard a sermon. "He isn't even baptized," it was whispered. He instilled the fear of an antichrist. On Good Friday, the knight joyfully proposed to his companions that they feast and then to go hunting. But

this time, the other guests refused in spite of the terror he inspired in them.

"Today is Good Friday, Sir, the day that Christ underwent crucifixion. We can neither eat nor go hunting on this day. It would be blasphemy."

"I don't care about that." He drew his sword and asked, "Are you going to eat with me?"

In a predicament, they accepted unwillingly, and the companions took their places at the table. They ate in silence and in great affliction, as if each mouthful burned their throats. After the meal they mounted their horses.

In the heart of the forest stood a small chapel where a hermit lived. The holy man knew the knight and prayed to God every day that the knight's bloodthirsty fury might be appeased.

The companions riding past the chapel pulled on their horses' bridles and turned toward the knight.

"Would you be so good as to allow us to pause here, Sir? At least on this Good Friday we would like to confess our sins."

"Go ahead. But be quick about it!" replied the knight.

He could not persuade his entire company, but he was sickened by them. He moved away a little so that he couldn't see the cross.

But the hermit saint came out of the chapel and accosted him.

"Good day, Sir. May peace be with you!"

"Peace? No thanks, for I don't want peace."

"What, even on this holy day you commit blasphemy?"

"I didn't realize it. But since you insist, yes, I have committed blasphemy, and your God doesn't frighten me."

The holy man cast him an odd look.

"I can see that your soul has gone astray. You ought to confess and repent."

The knight laughed in his face and turned his horse away, but the priest persisted.

"It grieves me to see your heart is so hard. You can't continue to damn yourself like this."

"I will damn myself as much as I wish, and do not say another word or you will be the first one to die."

"Don't you want to confess your sins?"

"No!"

"Or even say a simple prayer?"

"I have never said a prayer."

"Not even an amen?"

"Leave me! Understood?" retorted the knight, drawing his sword.

The hermit pondered.

"Could you at least take this keg and go and fetch some water for me? Unless it is beyond your strength."

The knight looked at the small keg and, further away, the clear river that flowed.

"That much I can do," he replied, sniggering.

If he were to atone for his crimes by carrying out this small favor, he could earn favor with God.

He dismounted, took the little bucket, and dipped it into the water. But not a drop of water would go in. He withdrew the bucket as empty as it was before.

"This is witchcraft!" exclaimed the knight.

"I have never come across such a hard-hearted man," replied the hermit. "You haven't even captured a single drop in the keg. A child in your place would have brought it back brimming with water."

The knight swore and cursed, but still did not ask for help from his companions. His jaw was tense. He took the keg again:

"I will not give up. I swear I will take it back filled."

He motioned to his companions to go their own way, and he spurred his horse.

He stopped at the first spring he found and dipped the little keg into it, but it would not fill. In a violent temper, he held it under the water for some time, as if to drown it, but the keg came out as empty as it was when it went in. The knight cursed and shouted in fury, but continued on his way.

Soon there was not one spring in the country, whether pond, river, or stream, that he had not visited. One day his horse dropped dead and he had to continue on foot with the keg around his neck. He had no money, for he was neither a lord nor a merchant.

Since leaving, he had depleted all his resources. He fed on fruit from the trees and stalks of grain. He slept in barns and haystacks. Sometimes a peasant would threaten him with a pitchfork and he had to make his bed under the hedgerows.

He crossed into Italy, almost an island surrounded by water. He held the keg submerged in seawater for so long the salt affected his skin.

After some years the former knight was no longer recognizable. He'd had to swap his magnificent clothes for rags found along the way. He was thin and haggard; his bones were poking through his skin. His eyebrows had grown thick, his eyes sunken. He seldom spoke, he moved with great difficulty, and the keg that had once seemed light to him weighed around his neck like a lintel.

Finally he decided to go back to the chapel. He was going to return to the hermit the accursed keg which he had never been able to fill with the slightest drop of water from any known source in the world.

Since a great deal of strength was required for the return journey, the knight was weary when he arrived. He dropped from exhaustion on the path leading to the retreat of the holy hermit, who had to run and set him on his feet again. The hermit accompanied the knight to the chapel and laid him down before the cross.

"I recognized my keg," said the holy man. "Who gave it to you? I gave it to a knight ages ago."

"I am that knight," he babbled. "I have roamed the world, I have been as far as the Black Sea. You have driven me mad with your keg. It never filled with a single drop. And I feel I shall not live much longer."

Then the knight noticed that the holy hermit was flustered, that he cried, wept, and invoked God for him with his whole soul. He saw that the hermit was so zealous that the knight was disconcerted. His distress moved him. Why was this man, whom he hardly knew, taking such care of him?

"Now, confess," said the hermit saint. "Now or never. You are on the threshold of the eternal Kingdom."

The knight surrendered. He stated his murders, crimes, thefts, pillages. For years he had tormented the peasants.

They used to call him the devil, a reputation he enjoyed. His wish was to be feared, and he had feared to be loved. But suddenly he understood. He felt the suffering of those he had persecuted. Thanks to his years of restless wandering, his soul was ready to open. His heart was softened by a flame. Love surged in him—a love that found its outlet in a tear in the corner of his eye. It ran down his cheek and fell as a sheer drop into the bucket.

And . . . a miracle! This keg that no water had been able to penetrate was filled entirely by a tear.

"You see. You who could not give anything because you were unable to take anything. As soon as you have received, you have given. Your soul is now at rest."

The knight with the keg went to sleep rather than died.

Three Pieces of Advice from a Bird

A man caught a small bird. "I am no use to you as a captive," the bird said to him, "but give me back my freedom and I will give you three pieces of advice that will be more useful than the miserable scrap of flesh that you might garner from my small body."

The bird said it would give the first piece of advice while still in the man's hand, the second from a nearby branch, and the third from the top of the mountain.

The winged creature was scrawny, so the man accepted. The bird's first piece of advice was this: "If you lose something— even if you value it as much as your life—do not be distressed."

The man released the bird, which then settled on a branch. It ruffled its feathers and said, "Here is my second piece of advice:

Never believe without evidence anything which is contrary to common sense."

The man grunted.

"What foolish remarks. This advice is commonplace."

Having finally reached the mountain top, the bird said:

"What a shame! My body conceals two enormous precious stones. If you had killed me they would have been yours!"

The man stamped his foot, pulled his hair out, rolled in the grass, and shouted:

"Bird, you have well and truly swindled me when you could have made me supremely happy! Mind I don't catch you again!"

But all of a sudden he stopped.

"And the third piece of advice? You owe me another one, you thief!"

"Imbecile," replied the bird, "you want a third piece of advice when you have not paid the least bit of attention to the first two. I told you not to fret if you lose something and not to believe things that contradict

common sense. Now you are upset about having lost two enormous precious stones, when all you had to do was look at me to see that my body could contain just one small jewel at most!"

Whereupon the bird flew away, free at last from any further concern with its appearance.

The Miser

Once upon a time there was a miser, a man whose hands were shaped like an eagle's claws. The moment he held anything, he was unable to let it go. This was useful for grabbing hold of branches if he fell from trees, but painful if he grasped a poker the wrong way.

If his stomach had functioned the way his money did, it would have split as soon as he was born, like a bag bursting at the seams. And yet his avarice ruined even his health, for the larger his nest egg grew, the more worn out the merchant became. In fact, he constantly checked his stash of money; he no longer slept or ate, as he was so anxious about its security.

However, one night in the small hours an idea occurred to him. In his shed there was a wooden log so heavy he could hardly move it. He drilled a small hole in the log and buried the coins inside. Then he covered the big log with other logs.

This strategy merely served to displace the problem. Rather than watching his coins closely, he kept a close eye on his log and was exceedingly careful whenever he lit a fire at home.

But he was on his guard against fire when it was water he should have feared.

One evening a month later, as the miser was on his way upstairs to bed, a storm broke. First came the lightning, streaking the sky, followed by a rolling of thunder, which brought rain. The water that had been contained for so long in the steel grey clouds flowed at once in a powerful flood. Streets became rivers, puddles became lakes, and houses became boats. The logs in the merchant's shed were carried away by a strong current.

The storm did not subside until the morning. The blessed dawn lit the scattered remains of the storm. Torn roofs; wrecked sheds. The log had been swept out of the shed and landed a few miles further on, in front of a blacksmith's house. As the blacksmith left his house he spotted the sizeable log and, overjoyed, he dragged it under the roof to chop for firewood. The first blow of the axe revealed the treasure inside. He called his wife and two daughters and showed them what the storm had carried their way to relieve them of their misery.

Meanwhile the miser lay half-dead before the sight of his destroyed shed. However, he recovered and swore that unless he found his possession he would never to go home again.

He turned into the sunken path which had been hollowed out by the storm during the night.

In each village he went to the inn and asked:

"You wouldn't have heard about a log as wide as a barrel?"

Everyone poked fun at him.

The story of the man who went chasing after his log spread everywhere. The rumor was swift and reached the village of the blacksmith, who understood and did not laugh.

The miser returned to his village.

The peasants were waiting for him in the inn. They were already laughing.

"Is it you who has lost a log?"

"Yes. Last year I lost the rim of my well!"

"Oh. Don't mention it," said the butcher, "Just two weeks ago I couldn't find my butcher's block."

"And, as for me," said the joiner, "From these substantial planks I made a brand new piece of timber."

"As for the anvil of the ...!"

"The anvil is in its place," said the blacksmith, who had just entered.

Those who were laughing fell silent and glanced at the spoilsport.

The blacksmith was honest, but not stupid.

He wished to put the merchant to the test in order to know the Creator's will.

In the kitchen his wife was preparing loaves. He had an idea. He asked her to bake three extra loaves: a large one, one of medium thickness, and a small one. He also asked her to prepare a festive breakfast.

The following day the miser arrived. He asked to be shown around the house. The blacksmith had been expecting him and removed the coins from the log. Only twigs and sticks were to be found under his roof.

The merchant sat down and said he had no appetite. However, he did the meal credit and cast his host sidelong glances; he did not understand the blacksmith's generosity. Just as he was about to leave, the blacksmith showed him the three loaves his wife had baked and suggested he try one. The largest was stuffed with earth, the middle-sized one contained a bone, and the small one was filled with the money found in the block.

The miser chose the biggest and heaviest loaf.

"But this is the most substantial one; the wheat is better and is more nourishing," said the blacksmith, pointing to the smallest loaf.

The miser would not give up. He clutched the large loaf firmly and was unwilling to release it from his grasp.

"Such is your decision," said the blacksmith. He watched him leave.

For once, the money went to the poverty-stricken. For once, money was outsmarted.

The Clothes Chest

Father Poemen used to say, "If you have a chest full of clothes and do not open it for a long time, the clothes inside will go moldy."

The same is true of the thoughts in our heart. If we do not act upon them, they eventually spoil and change for the worse.

Saint Francis and the Wolf

Francis loved animals. He saw a sacred link between animals and men and spoke to all his brothers in the same way, whether they were feathered or furred, and whether they walked upright or on all fours.

One day Francis was on his way to the abbey of Gubbio. He walked at a brisk pace, leading his donkey by its bridle. Just as he began to see the towers of the abbey coming into view above the trees, his path was blocked by some peasants.

"Brother Francis, do not go any further! Ferocious wolves are prowling around. They are starving and will devour you if you go on!"

"I have not hurt them at all and neither has my soul. Don't worry. Return to God! Good night."

Francis then passed by the peasants quite peacefully and plunged into the forest along the dark road. He was not worried about the wolves.

He appeared at the gate of the town of Gubbio. Oddly, it was shut. Some guards half-opened it, allowed Francis through, and closed it quickly behind them. The brother wished to rest, but the townspeople crowded together and bombarded him with questions:

"Have you seen the wolves?"

"And above all the most terrible one, a grey wolf, almost black."

"It is rabid."

"We no longer dare to go out," moaned a mother, her child in her arms.

"It killed someone last week . . . ," shrieked the surviving companion.

"Yes. It kills and pursues everything it finds, but it is never satisfied!"

"It is a devil!" exclaimed a terror-stricken old woman.

Francis raised his hands as a sign of reassurance. When silence fell anew he just said:

"I am going to leave and speak with the wolf."

The townspeople stifled their cries, but no one dared to utter anything.

When the slender saint slipped through the gap of the open door some people were already praying that his soul might rest in peace.

He did not go far. At the edge of the wood the wolf suddenly appeared, with his mouth open. He slavered, lips curled up on his bared fangs.

Francis made the sign of the cross and sat down calmly on a stump.

"Come near me, brother wolf."

Surprised, the wolf shut his mouth. He approached with measured steps and sat down.

"I have heard that you sow terror hereabout. And you see that you devastate and devour and yet you are always hungry!"

The wolf whined.

"I understand the people of Gubbio are afraid of you and want your hide. But I would like to reconcile you both so you no longer fear men or their dogs."

From the heights of the city walls the citizens, dumbfounded, observed the holy man talking to the wolf.

"If you make peace, brother wolf, I promise that the people will feed you every day until you die. It is hunger that drives you mad. If you promise to do no more harm, you will be looked after."

The wolf observed the man, and took an especially good look at his eyes. He saw that the words were sound and that his soul was in harmony with them. The wolf felt loved as a creature endowed with wit and reason. He approached Francis, lowered his head, and placed his paw in his hand.

The brother stroked his rough fur. Then he stood up and the wolf followed him. He walked toward the city walls with the wolf at his heel. And Francis entered the town with the wolf at his side. He didn't meet anyone.

Frightened, the habitants had taken refuge behind their walls and well-locked doors.

In the main square, Saint Francis spoke. He told the people of Gubbio that they were so grasping that they refused to feed even a wolf. And that the wolf took revenge. But if they were to give the wolf the wherewithal to satisfy hunger, he would stop wreaking havoc.

As a token of agreement, the animal sat back on its haunches before the saint and licked his sandals. Then the townspeople dared to surface. The wolf looked at them without stirring.

The townspeople prostrated themselves before the saint and promised to feed the animal every day and, if it were ill, even to care for it. Brother Francis blessed the men and the wolf.

For the two years the wolf lived, he respected his promise and received his sustenance every day. He entered houses as if he were at home. Even the dogs welcomed him as one of their own. When he died from old age, the townspeople wept for him and followed his mortal remains while the bell tolled.

Pope Gregory

The Golden Legend

After a gilded youth, Saint Gregory had chosen to retire behind the quiet walls of a monastery. However, one day a shipwrecked man came to him.

The man complained that after having been shipwrecked he was completely penniless and had to beg to survive. Gregory gave him six silver deniers. On the evening of the same day, the shipwrecked man returned and said that he had lost a great deal, but received too little. Gregory gave to him all the remaining money in the monastery. The beggar returned for a third time, hurled abuse at the monks, and accused them of keeping the best for themselves. Now the monastery was empty. It no longer contained anything precious apart from a silver bowl—a present from

Gregory's mother—which was used to carry vegetables. The shipwrecked man's insults notwithstanding, Gregory gave him the dish.

Many years later, Gregory was elected pope. He had in no way sought this election. In order to avoid this honor he had fled to Rome, hidden in a cask. But a column of fire, descending from heaven, had indicated his hiding place and he had to return to be consecrated.

This burden weighed upon him. He dreamt with delight of his monastery, his prayers, and the silence of the cloister: "I consider what I have lost: here I am battered by the waves of an immense sea, while in the vessel of my soul I am broken by the raging of a dreadful storm. When I look back on my life, I sigh as if I were turning my gaze toward the receding shore." While Gregory was pondering nostalgically, his counselor showed in the twelve pilgrims whom he always used to welcome at his table on Fridays. They were all seated and thoroughly enjoying a feast of delicious dishes served on silver plates. Gregory checked how many there were, but instead of twelve he counted thirteen plates. He complained to his counselor, who counted them again and only found twelve. On checking once more, Gregory found thirteen. Amongst the guests he suddenly noticed a man whose face changed. Now he was young; now old; now bearded; now clean-shaven. Struck by this marvel, Gregory stared, dumbfounded.

The man then revealed himself and assumed his real form, which was that of an angel with white wings. He addressed Gregory:

"Recognize in me the shipwrecked man who once knocked three times at the door of your monastery. You gave me everything. To you as well, shipwrecked in honor, and buffeted by the waves of the world, I also give everything."

The angel flew away, haloing Gregory with the rapture of the Blessed ones.

The Hermit's Cat

In the time of Pope Gregory, a hermit lived in the forest. This holy man's only company was a small white cat. He stroked it often, holding it on his lap like a lady companion.

One night he was on his knees and prayed to God to reveal to him the person with whom he would share his final resting-place. In the morning a dream revealed to him that he might hope to share it with Pope Gregory.

Suddenly the hermit woke up and kneeled anew on his *prie-dieu*, rebellious and protesting:

"My poverty, which I chose, and for many years have embraced, is of little use to me when I raise myself no higher than a rich man laden with honors."

Life went on, yet the hermit was still troubled. He could not stop comparing his poverty to Gregory's riches. One night he dreamt that God was speaking with him again. He heard him say:

"It is not the possession of riches, but lust for them that makes one rich. You who cling to your cat are richer than Gregory who gives everything he possesses unstintingly. You take greater pleasure in stroking your cat than he does in profiting from the wealth that is useless to him."

Lying

Jesus said, "Do not tell lies! Do not do what you hate, for you are naked before heaven. That which you conceal and that which is veiled: everything will be disclosed."

The Monk's Three Sins

A monk felt resentment toward the abbot of the monastery. Unable to rid himself of this aggression—rather the reverse—he brooded over it, justifying it and making excuses; thus, the hatred increased rapidly. In the solitude of his cell he was assailed by a terrible thought: He wished to see the abbot dead.

Hardly had this thought taken root in his mind than the abbot had an apoplectic fit. He collapsed and died forthwith. That very evening the Devil appeared to the monk. He greeted the monk, but the poor brother did not reply. He moaned, wrung his hands, rolled on the ground, and blamed himself for this vile act.

The Devil deployed all his artifices, but the monk could not be persuaded.

The horned beast had to raise his voice:

"Hey! I answered your prayers, so be pleased!"

To give force to his statements, he spat a tongue of fire. Finally the monk, looking distraught, raised his head.

"It is your turn to do something for me," Satan continued. "As payment for my services I compel you to sin. Out of these three sins, choose yours: drink, fornicate, or kill!"

The wretched monk, who was greatly vexed by all this, bargained for some time. But the Devil was inflexible. If the monk refused, the Devil would make do with making his crime of thought public. Having run out of arguments, the monk chose the lesser of the sins that the Devil had offered: drink.

Once when he was slightly tipsy he whispered sweet nothings into a lady's ear. As she pushed him away he hitched up her skirt. He was on the verge of ecstasy when the husband appeared. To silence him, the monk killed him.

Rather than one crime, he committed three.

The Misdeed

A brother of Scetis committed a misdeed that is omitted in history books. However, it was considered sufficiently serious for the elders to meet in order to decide on a punishment for the sinning monk. To ensure the greatest justice they called Father Moses, inviting him to sit with them.

At first the abbot refused to come. But once he received several messages from the Scetis fathers he set off. He took an old bag riddled with holes and filled with sand, dragging it behind him through the desert.

From the rooftop of the monastery, one of the Scetis monks saw the abbot coming over the hill. As he walked with difficulty, everyone hurried to help him.

One of the elders caught sight of the bag and asked, "Why are you laden with a bag of sand?"

"My misdeeds follow behind me and I cannot see them," said Father Moses. "And today you ask me to judge someone else's misdemeanors."

The elders bowed their heads to honor those elders even older than them.

What Jesus Said About the Clean and Unclean

Gospel of Thomas

"There is nothing outside man that, entering him, can soil him. But what issues forth from man is what soils him. Whoever has ears, let him hear."

At a distance from the crowd, he added these words for his disciples:

"Whatever enters the body of man does not go in his heart, but in his belly and leaves with ease. But what man nourishes in his heart, perverse intentions, theft, debauchery, trickery, defamation—all this comes from inside and soils men."

Laundry

Jesus and Saint Peter, passing through a village, asked some poor people for hospitality that night. The man and woman warmly welcomed the pilgrims, laying out before them all their remaining provisions.

The next day, Jesus, who was well rested, asked his hosts what their day's task was.

"A little laundry," replied the man, "for the people in the village."

"May the work you begin in the morning last you until the evening," said Jesus.

"My God, that would surprise me," exclaimed the woman, "We have only a few shirts to wash."

But Jesus insisted, "May power be to my word!"

And indeed, the word wrought this miracle: The good people washed and washed and the linen sack seemed always to be full. They lifted piles of clean cotton clothing and there was hardly any room left to stack all the shirts from the tub.

Their neighbors watched this never-ending laundry from their windows and wondered what accounted for such activity.

The same evening, through a few insidious questions, the neighbor learned of the visit and the pilgrims' astonishing prediction.

As Jesus and Saint Peter had been on the road since the morning, the neighbor and his wife hopped into their cart and hurtled along the road to catch up with them. Finally they saw them and exclaimed:

"Lords. Surely you aren't going to leave our village already! Rest in our house, you will be better off taking to the road again tomorrow!"

Jesus observed them and accepted, and everyone returned to the village in the cart, drawn by a horse blind in one eye. The neighbor and his wife were skinflints. They served Jesus and Saint Peter with measured generosity.

After a difficult night because of a lumpy mattress, Jesus asked his hosts what their job of the day was.

"Lord, it is the day of the accounts," said the woman raising her eyes skyward.

"The work you begin this morning will last you throughout the day," said Jesus.

"Oh, it won't take long," said the woman innocently. We only have a few measly coins."

"May power be to my word."

The misers were already rubbing their hands and pressing their fingers together industriously so that the piles might grow quickly.

But before getting down to it, they went to the lavatory.

And the work begun that morning continued until the evening, when, furious, their backsides in a state of discomfiture, they were at last able to extricate themselves from the throne.

Saint Peter
Beaten Twice

Jesus and Saint Peter had taken up lodgings at a farm as day laborers.

When morning broke, the farmer got up early to see whether his new recruits were in the fields. He looked for them everywhere without success. Finally he glanced in the bedroom and found them sprawled on their straw mattresses. Jesus was sleeping next to the wall and it was Saint Peter, lying on the edge of the bed, who received the flogging.

Jesus got up as if nothing had happened, stretched, and yawned. Saint Peter, extensively bruised, painfully stretched his limbs and, without a word, followed his Lord to the field.

At nightfall, however, he said to Jesus that he would prefer to sleep on the wall side.

"The wall is dreadfully damp and unhealthy, Lord. It is right that I suffer from it too."

Just like the day before, the next morning they did not wake, whereas the

other laborers had been working since dawn. The master seized his stick angrily and ran to their bedroom. At the sight of the two men slouched, sleeping the sleep of the just, he unleashed his anger. He raised his stick, but suddenly realized that the previous day he had beaten the man on the edge. So he decided to lay into the man who was sleeping on the wall side. Saint Peter received a beating for the second time. He got up, bruised and battered, and again said nothing.

But in the evening when they went to bed, irritably he said:

"Sleep wherever you wish, my Lord. In all events it is I who will be flogged."

"Not if you know how to keep your place," answered Jesus.

Abbot John Recounted This...

A Greek philosopher instructed one of his disciples to let himself be insulted when the opportunity arose and even to pay his offenders. After three years of being put to the test, the master said:

"Now you are ready. You can go to Athens and acquire knowledge from the masters."

The disciple left.

Strolling under the Athenian columns, the disciple noticed a sage who was insulting all the passers-by. The sage also insulted the disciple, who gave him a coin. He threw it back in the disciple's face, whereupon the young man started to laugh.

"Why do you laugh?" asked the sage.

"For three years I have paid to be insulted and you do it for nothing."

"Come and sit next to me," answered the sage. "The city belongs to you."

And Abbot John added these words:

"Here is the Gate through which our Fathers entered the celestial city."

Saint Peter's Mother

During her life, Saint Peter's mother had been an absolute termagant. Spiteful, scolding, given to lying and stealing, she had accumulated so many defects that on her death, despite the indulgence granted to her on family grounds, God refused to admit her to paradise.

Saint Peter was now dispirited; he wandered among the flowerbeds where the flowers blossomed; he heaved sighs which could have cleaved stones even if in this place he was the only stone. God finally realized his distress and asked him:

"Peter, my dear fellow, you know you can confide in me. Tell me what saddens you."

"Lord, how can I be happy here when I know that my mother endures the most terrible torture in hell?"

God felt embarrassed.

"Yes . . . of course, but your mother . . . All right then. Listen, Peter," he concluded, "During her life did your mother perform a single praiseworthy action? Seek and if you find one, however small, I swear to you I will let her come here."

Saint Peter went forthwith to the vast library in Paradise where the books of the souls since Adam and Eve were conserved. The shelves rose as high as the peaks of the clouds. He looked for the book concerning his mother. It was a large volume, for she had lived to a ripe old age. He placed it on a table of stardust, revived a few fireflies and began to read.

He blanched, sighed, twisted his mouth, and covered his eyes out of fear of what he was reading. Several times he closed the book to rest his frightened spirit. Then, full of courage, he resolutely continued the detailed account of his mother's dark actions. Just as he was about to lose hope, he suddenly leapt up from his well-padded seat and exclaimed triumphantly:

"Lord, Lord! I have found it. One day she gave a leek leaf to a penniless man who was dying of hunger."

"Ah. Good," sighed God, "That will do. This leek leaf will save her."

Saint Peter gently removed the leek leaf from the memory book and let it flutter down from paradise. The thin leaf became longer and longer. It drifted into a smoking chimney stack that led to the balcony of glowing embers, finally reaching Hell. Saint Peter's mother was sweeping glowing coals. She was the first to see the leaf drift down.

She leapt up, caught it, kept tight hold of it, and impatiently began to lift herself up on it. Raising her gaze, she noticed her son waving to her from high up in heaven. The sight of his snow-white hair mingled with the frothy clouds emboldened her, and the old woman climbed with amazing speed. But suddenly, on glancing below, she noticed other damned souls who had also seized the opportunity and were following her.

"This leak leaf is mine! Stop! It will break," exclaimed the old woman.

But her cries did not deter them. They climbed up, clinging to the slim hope of salvation. Saint Peter's mother suddenly halted. Waiting until they were within her reach, she began to nudge with her heel all those who had caught up with her. One by one she forced her pursuers to fall back down to Hell.

Her son, who was watching her, wept.

When the old woman was sure that she was at last the only one to be saved, the leaf gave way.

The Tale of the Fellow Masons

Once upon a time there were two industrious fellow masons who got through a lot of work. They always traveled together and spent most of their time on roofs and scaffolding rather than on firm ground.

One enjoyed cards and was constantly on the lookout for an opportunity to play a game, whereas the other had a predilection for the bottle. In the evening he drank like a fish, became more saturated than a sponge, came home in a rage, and beat his wife and children.

One evening while the first journeyman was at home, he heard a knock on the door. It was an old pilgrim in a threadbare coat who asked for shelter that night.

"Come in and sit down," said the mason, ushering him in.

"But I am not alone."

"Well, call your mate."

"But there are twelve of us."

"Twelve! When there is not even enough room for one!"

The journeyman's wife served soup to the guests and found a bed in the barn for each man. The next morning, the mason refused to let them leave on an empty stomach, and his wife filled each bowl with some soup and offered a piece of bread.

"God will pay you back," said the man seated at the center. "What would you like?"

"What I would really like—my most cherished desire—is to win the game."

"Let it be."

And this happened. From that day on he no longer lost. But he liked his job as a mason and continued to spend more time on cornices than in taverns, whereas his friend became tipsier every day and more terrible every evening.

One day the two masons had to repair the church tower. They were perched there when suddenly the scaffolding gave way. They came crashing down with beams, plaster, and stone; they fell onto the cobblestones of the square.

"My friend. I'm dead," said the gambler. "I'm going to heaven."

"Me too, I'm dead," replied the drunkard. "But where will I go?"

"Do you regret all those blows and your dreadful booze-ups?"

"Now that I'm dead I do, yes. But what's the point now?"

Then the lame one, the horned Devil, unexpectedly arrived. He was about to lead the drunkard away when the gambler intervened:

"Wait. It's soul for soul. Have a game with me and win two souls or lose them."

The Devil smiled and accepted. He was sure he would win. And while no one knew how it happened, the friend won. He had a good patron. The Devil had to release the soul that for such a long time had been his.

The gambler led his friend to the gates of paradise. Saint Peter wouldn't hear of the drunkard. But the other man exclaimed that he would not enter without him. "He has mended his ways," he repeated.

The rumor drew the attention of the good Lord.

"What's going on here?"

"I don't want to enter without him," said the gambler.

"You only asked me that you might win a game of cards. Why should I accept both of you?"

"Because there are two of us. Because we are close. That's why the Devil couldn't take us."

God heard and opened wide the gates of paradise for them.

The Call

One morning Abbot John Colombos suddenly sat up in his bed. He was bathed in sweat, an acrid sweat. To his elder brother, who was sharing his cell, he said:

"I have had enough. I want to live as an angel, without working, but in the relentless service of God."

He took all his clothes off, left the building, and set forth into the desert. A week later, insistent knocks were heard at the monastery door.

"Who's there?" asked the monk who was on the other side.

"It's John."

"Which John?"

"John Colombos."

"It's not possible. My brother has turned into an angel. He's no longer amongst men."

"Yes. It's me, John. Let me in, I beg you."

"I pray every day for my brother who is in the relentless service of God."

"Are you going to let me in, you clot?"

But the older brother refused to recognize him and left him outside.

Eventually, when John was too weary to knock on the wooden door, his older brother said to him:

"If you are an angel, why do you shut yourself up in a cell? If you are a man, you should work as men do."

"That's true," replied John. "Forgive me, my brother, and let me in."

The Workaholic

There was once a blacksmith who worked constantly and with tenacity. He would get up at daybreak and go to bed without caring about the setting sun. He forgot about all other duties. He neglected pleasure and scorned nourishment from the earth. He did not have a single day off. He took no time to admire the wind that whistled at the windowpane or taste the flavor of a simmering soup.

On Sundays, when everyone was relaxing, enjoying themselves, or lying down in the fields, the blacksmith was at his smithy.

When his death hour came, Saint Peter inquired of the Lord:

"Does this fellow deserve to enter paradise? He hasn't done wrong, and he has worked so hard!"

"He has worked too hard," replied

God bad-temperedly. "He may have done nothing wrong, but neither has he done anything good . . . And, after all, didn't I myself rest?"

"But you can't deny his courage and tenacity," insisted Saint Peter.

"All right," said God. "I accept him. But only if he manages to hoist himself up by his tool."

Saint Peter, irritated, kept his gaze on heaven (he could not raise his eyes, for he was already at the summit). Then he leaned over and extended his arms to the earth where the blacksmith lay.

With a decisive gesture he seized the blacksmith's tool. It was an enormous hammer, a formidable block fashioned in iron deeply sunken into the boxwood handle. As soon as the saint picked up the hammer, the blacksmith straightened up and clung to it. Saint Peter pulled. In this way he hauled the blacksmith toward paradise. But midway between earth and Heaven the hammer, which had always bent metal, cracked and broke. The split ran along the entire length of the tool, breaking it. Saint Peter kept hold of the head of the hammer, while the blacksmith, hanging onto the handle, fell into the abyss.

Saint Peter uttered a cry. God suddenly appeared at his side and looked over his shoulder.

"The tool was more loved than I was," he said. "Come, Peter. If he is a blacksmith and loves his trade, won't he be happier down below?"

Recreation

Abbot Anthony was sitting in the shade with his monastic brothers. He was engaged in cheerful conversation and laughter when a hunter in pursuit of game appeared. On finding the monks so relaxed, the hunter was shocked and said to the abbot:

"Is this how you aim to serve God?"

The abbot asked him to bend his bow back and to shoot an arrow, then to do it again and again.

After a while the hunter lowered his weapon and muttered:

"If I stretch my bow like this, in the end it will break."

"And we are just the same," answered Anthony. "If we never slacken our devotions, we too will break."

Saint Vincent

S aint Vincent was the patron of wine-growers. In the second century, when this story unfolds, winegrowers were not yet very well organized; their work was sometimes characterized by considerable chaos, the effects of which were evident in the wine. But Vincent was gifted, his vines were superb and his wine ... divine. So the other winegrowers naturally chose him as their patron.

One day Vincent decanted the new wine from the vat and tasted it. Pleased, and with his taste buds still quivering, he invited his fellow winegrowers to drink with him. The winegrowers were delighted; they left their barrels forthwith and went to quench their thirst at Saint Vincent's vat. At first they tasted, then they drank, becoming intoxicated, and merrier and merrier, and more and more disorderly. The revelry was well advanced when a messenger appeared under the trellis. He had just undertaken a long journey under the sun and was parched.

Vincent welcomed him with a slap on the back and served him a goblet.

Now, the messenger was none other than the beneficent God himself. He wanted to know what the wine from the vine tasted like, since it looked so green on the hillside and exerted so strange an effect. He tasted it, assessed it, and poured himself another goblet. After several rounds the beneficent God unfastened his waistcoat and began to yell like the others:

"How high this mountain is and how good this new wine is!"

After a few casks, each man returned home, following a straight line that God, it is said, sometimes makes curved. And God, no less rolling, utterly drunk, set off again along the paths. Eventually he fell asleep on his feet in a vineyard and, snoozing away, fell to the ground.

Upon awaking the next day his forehead felt heavy. The sky was hazy. He nonetheless felt sufficiently cheerful in disposition to return and see Vincent.

This time he forgot to transform himself and he appeared in the full radiance of His Majesty. Vincent, dumbfounded, threw himself at his feet. After the night they had just spent, he feared the wrath of the Almighty Father toward his vines.

For his part, God tried to know more about the vine whose delicious juice had caused such a sweet dizziness.

"What is the name of this plant?"

Vincent thought for a moment and preferred to betray God rather than the winegrowers. He stated confidently:

"It is bramble, Lord."

Whereupon God, amazed, made this reply:

"Bramble will take root at both ends; it will multiply without needing to be planted and you will never be short of it. Let it be!"

Saint Peter's Lie

As they went along, Peter was gazing out at the verdant countryside, which stretched far and wide on all sides before disappearing into a mist. Suddenly he tugged on Christ's sleeve and said, "I have just seen an enormous hare, gigantic, as big as a horse." Christ answered him calmly that they were soon going to cross a special bridge that liars were unable to cross because they would fall into the water. The closer they came to this bridge, the smaller Saint Peter's hare became, until it was no bigger than a hare.

The Foundry Worker

A soldier was returning from war. He had aged considerably; his skin was pockmarked with bullets that had grazed him and his uniform was full of holes made by bullets that had hit him. Having left home at a young age he had aged twenty years. During all these years the only trade he had learned was that of holding a crossbow; he knew better how to stroke his weapon than a girl's knee.

He nonetheless dreamed of marrying and finding a good job. As he got closer

to his home he looked anxiously at the lovely stone bridges and the streams of his land. Would he be able to adjust to this peacefulness?

"Good morning, friend," came a voice from behind him.

He turned round and saw a spry old man smiling at him.

"So, are you coming back?"

"Yes. This time it's the retreat."

"If you are going this way we can continue together."

"Fine."

"And what's your name?"

"Nicholas."

"Fancy that! What a stroke of luck! They also call me Nicholas." Along the way they halted near a river. Old Nicholas caught three fish, which he gave to his companion to cook. Then the old man fell asleep, instructing the soldier not to touch the fried fish. But the pleasant aroma began to spread and overwhelmed the senses of the soldier. He paid no heed to the prohibition and without waking his accomplice he loosened the tender flesh from the first fish. The old man slept on, so the soldier continued eating. He gobbled up the second fish. He had hardly finished the last mouthful when the old man opened an eye:

"I note you didn't wake me ... but there's only one fish left ... where is the third one?"

"Which one?"

"You ate your portion and that one's mine, but where is the third fish?"

"I dozed off a little. Someone must have seen it and eaten it."

Without a word, old Nicholas tied a knot in his bag and set off again eating his fish. After a few miles he broke the silence:

"What do you know how to do?" he asked his companion. "You need to think about earning a penny or two."

"Oh!" the soldier exclaimed, "I can do everything. I am very skilled. I can even thread a needle with one hand!"

"All right, all right. We could try the trade of foundry worker."

"What's that? What's a foundry worker?"

"It's simple. It's like old pieces of metal. You melt down an old object, such as a scrap of metal, to make a new one."

"Really?"

"It's not difficult. You'll see."

They entered a town and old Nicholas shouted in the square:

"Casters of old things ... old things to cast ..."

In the main street there lived an old woman whose trembling made the remaining teeth in her mouth clink. She heard the two men:

"Go and take a look," she said to her servant, Manon.

And with that the two Nicholases appeared at the door of her room.

"What do you mean by your 'old things'?" asked the old woman.

"Well," replied old Nicholas, "after melting you, we return you to your good-looking twenty-year-old self."

"Oh," exclaimed the old woman, "is that possible? And how much does that cost?"

"Three thousand francs."

"If it is true, it's a gift! Come on, Manon, follow this gentleman's instructions carefully."

Old Nicolas filled a basin of boiling water in the courtyard. Then, gently, he seized the old woman.

"It doesn't hurt, does it?" she asked, bracing herself above the bubbles.

"Not in the slightest," he said, and thereupon he immersed her in the boiling water.

She entered as readily as a fish in a pond. After a few minutes, old Nicholas put the fire out and removed the whitened bones from the basin. He dried them, placed them in a clean piece of linen, which he slung over his back, and walked round the cauldron singing. Eventually he went back to the old woman's room and tidily laid out all the bones. He took a deep breath and blew on them.

A ravishing sweet young girl appeared, rosy-skinned and in a flowery dress. She smiled timidly at them and told her servant kindly to pay her benefactor for the service rendered. The servant took time to comply. She looked with eyes as round as saucers at her old mistress who had turned into an innocent maiden once more. Then, with flattery, the young girl accompanied the two men to the door, showering them with presents.

"What a fine trade!" exclaimed the soldier, "Now that I have done it on others I will do it to myself!"

"Do you think you are capable of this already?" asked old Nicholas.

"Of course! I watched you very closely. I will do the same. Ah. What a fine trade! But we shouldn't compete with each other in such matters. Right. You go that way and I'll go the other way."

"If you like."

With this the soldier, throwing out his chest, disappeared into an alley and began to shout, "Founder of old things!"

There happened to live in this street an old woman, whom death must have forgotten, almost blind, half-deaf, quite crippled, and who flailed about in bed without ever finding rest. With her good ear she heard the soldier's cry and ordered her housemaid to send for him.

Nicholas swaggered into the room, promising the old woman youth; he savored the impression he made and asked for six thousand francs.

The old woman would have given everything to have her youth restored, so she accepted.

Self-assured, the soldier prepared a cauldron in the courtyard, filling it with boiling water. He lifted the old woman from her bed and immersed her. But things did not go as smoothly as he had seen them done before.

The old woman shrieked and cried, wriggling convulsively, jerking her arms and legs around. The pain was already restoring her youth, for she had not flung herself about like this for a long time. She screamed to be taken out and the soldier, scalded, constantly had to put back in arms or legs that kept emerging from the basin.

Eventually he won by sheer force, while the housemaid yelled like a squealing pig.

He turned toward her and gave her a withering glance. "Shut up. You will spoil everything." The servant resisted the temptation to wail. Nicholas waited for the water to cool and took out the blanched bones one by one. He dried them, walked around the cauldron, and went back up to the room. He arranged the bones on the bed very carefully and blew on them. But nothing happened. Neither an old nor a young woman appeared . . . only a heap of dead bones. The housemaid suddenly appeared in the room, saw the result, and ran to the balcony:

"This time I will not keep quiet!"

Indeed, she was heard from the most distant hills of the town:

"Murder! Murder! Help! Guards! Guards turn out!"

The soldier, bone white, hurried to the staircase and ran down it. On his way out he caught sight of the night watchmen pursuing him. He ran as fast as his legs could carry him, breathless and desperate.

The men had almost reached him when he ran into a man: it was old Nicholas.

"Friend . . . you must get me out of here. It's about an old woman who didn't let herself be melted down?"

"Oh no? So tell me, after all," resumed his companion. "I just wanted to ask you . . . regarding that third fish."

"What, the third fish? Is now that time?"

"Who stole it? Do you know?"

"No, I don't know. I was asleep. Friend, it's a matter of urgency!"

Seeing that the soldier refused to speak, old Nicholas lowered his head. The night watchmen were seizing his companion when he made a gesture of appeasement:

"Leave him! It's a simple mistake. Follow us."

He headed for the old woman's house. They all went up to her bedroom. The skeleton was lying on the bed. Then old Nicholas straightened out a small bone in the foot. And he blew on it.

An even more beautiful and younger girl than the first one appeared on the bed. "Yes. It's me!" she smiled, casting a mischievous look at her housemaid, who was a beauty.

She got up, swayed her hips as she approached her writing desk, and took out an amply filled purse. She came back and held it out to Nicholas:

"This is for you and not for him—that unskillful one who hurt me so much!"

"Many thanks, madam!"

The two men walked through the line of dumbfounded night watchmen. They crossed the town and walked in silence as far as the trees. The soldier, ashamed, limped. Finally the old man sat down on a stump.

"We'll share the money. Two women were transformed. Three and six are nine. Three thousand for you, three thousand for me, and three thousand for the one who ate the fish."

"Why are you dividing it up into three parts? There are only two of us."

"Three because there were three fish."

The soldier lowered his head and said:

"I'm the one who ate it."

"And now you own up to it in order to get the money!"

The old man looked him up and down, eyed him gravely; his look then softening.

"Be warned that I am Nicholas, your patron saint. So take all the money and start again. Go, act modestly, and do what you know you can do, get married and live in austerity. You'll feel well."

The soldier bowed and kissed the saint's feet. He took the gift and continued the path to the village. Along the way, the low sky seemed to embrace him.

Temptation

The desert fathers used to say, "If you are assailed by a temptation in the desert, do not forsake it while it lasts. For, if you flee in this way, you find it again wherever you go. Wait patiently until it vanishes.

Agatha's Absence

A nun called Agatha was the sister door-keeper at the monastery of Notre-Dame-de-la-Charité. She was in charge of watching the comings and goings at the threshold of the heavy oak door that closed the convent. After matins she would settle on the bench next to the door that, throughout the day, she opened and closed; in the evening, with a turn of the big key, she locked the entry to the monastery.

With the passing of time this task came to weigh upon her. It was in vain that she repeated to herself that her patron was Saint Peter, who relentlessly kept vigil at the gate of paradise; she found her life dreary and repetitive. After all, in the extravagance of the real world a concierge still talks, discusses, and observes. But in the convent, sister Agatha could not speak to the nuns who had taken a vow of silence and there was nothing for her to observe except for the oak door and the intersecting white drapes. And prayer was of no help because her body was numbed and her soul restless.

Soon she started to dream of being elsewhere. This insistent thought amidst a maelstrom of long-suppressed ideas became as wild and impulsive as a torrent. Elsewhere . . . anywhere . . . everything seemed more desirable than the job of gatekeeper, being trapped on the threshold, neither inside nor outside.

The idea finally morphed into a decision. The next morning the nun did not even sit on her stone bench. After opening the heavy oak door, she went back into the chapel and placed her key on the altar under the statue of the Virgin. She crossed herself, and fled without looking behind her, saw the horizon before her, sighed in relief, and, smiling, went down to the town.

Not wishing to be recognized, she did not linger in the upper part of town, as

the sisters visited from time to time. She
went to the lower part of the town, which
was teeming with rabble. Thieves, rapists
and murderers, bandits and loafers, and
pickpockets would meet in the taverns and
they were drunk until daybreak.

The nun was quick to flounder in this
seedy underworld, unable to cope with the
position she wished to occupy in the world.
A bandit who had no fear of heaven hitched
up her sackcloth. Without invitation he
entered her and was followed by many
others. They all crossed the threshold
without the slightest need for a key and
left when they had had their fill. No sooner
was the nun emancipated than she became
a lost girl.

After a while she withdrew into herself.
The former sister Agatha, who once
dreamed of talking about everything, could
not bear the gossip of the other prostitutes
and their pimps. Love, which had once
made her daydream, had become a torture
and she knew that from now on she was

destined for hell. In reality, she was already there. And she dreamed of her former life as a lost paradise. From the narrow road she no longer dared leave, she sometimes raised her gaze toward the convent with its white walls, belfry, and carefree sisters. But she did not dare return, for after her degeneration how would she be welcomed?

One evening, more despairing than ever, she drank to forget herself. For this she needed only a little brandy. She left the inn and staggered off. She wished to breathe in fresh air and to escape for a bit.

Thus, she ventured step by step beyond her territory. She walked along the path that connected the hill of the low town to the high town where the monastery stood. She must have been beside herself to carry out the folly she had dreamed of for so many months. She rang the bell at the monastery door. A nun opened the door for her and welcomed her warmly:

"Welcome, Sister Agatha."

She stood aside to let her in.

In the moonlight, Agatha could tell that the new sister doorkeeper resembled her exactly.

She suddenly sobered up and looked at the nun.

The lady smiled and was her old self again; the face of pure affection was framed by a blue veil. She then returned to heaven in the dark, toward the end of the night.

Mary the Holy Mother had taken her place. So, during her long absence no one had suspected that Agatha had run away.

The Wind

A brother came and saw Father Poemen and said to him:

"Father, when I pray I cannot control my thoughts. My head is full of distractions and I am afraid of endangering my salvation."

The old man caught the novice by his robe and left the tent. A violent wind brought down the canvas and whipped up the sand.

"Open your chest and hold in the wind."

To please the old man, the youth opened out his robe and the wind violently rushed in. But it didn't stop there.

"It's impossible, Father."

"You can no more prevent your mind becoming filled with distractions than you can hold in the wind. But you can avoid being blown away with it."

The Virgin's Mill

After having fought ten years as a soldier in the uprising, Simon returned home to his hill. His father had just died, bequeathing his mill to him. But this legacy was rather burdensome, for the mill fell into ruin, the blades were torn, some of the roof tiles and essential stonework were missing, and the millstone no longer turned. What's more, his poor father died penniless and had not settled his debts that, over time, had accumulated.

But Simon decided not to be disheartened. Delighted to have a mill and a plot of land, he got down to work. Although he couldn't read, he could do odd jobs, and soon the mill, repaired and whitewashed, stood out proudly on the hill.

Simon believed his courage would suffice to bring back happy days.

But the mill continued to be beset by ill-fortune. The wind could blow mercilessly for days, but as soon as the miller took control it suddenly stopped; the north wind unexpectedly ceased and the blades no longer turned. The poor miller was reduced to blowing on the motionless blades himself.

Was this ill-fortune or fate? In the end Simon thought God bore him a grudge. It was simply not possible for the wind alone to be so ill disposed!

Meanwhile, the debts continued to pile up. One day he received a notice, which said that unless he paid them the bailiff would come the next day and seize his mill.

That day the wind howled. As Simon watched the surrounding fields from the top of his mill he suddenly noticed down below Father Francis's cart, filled with wheat. He rushed out onto the road, unloaded the sacks, and exclaimed:

"It's for tomorrow, my Father, without fail. Can you imagine, in this wind . . . ?"

But his phrase remained hanging in the air. The wind! The wind had ceased. Suddenly, there was no longer the slightest breeze. The leaves were motionless. You had to crane your neck to breathe.

So Simon, exhausted, grumbled:

"If God is deaf, let the Devil hear me!"

No sooner was the Devil invoked than it came into view, wearing a smile.

The Devil promised Simon flour, fortune, and wind in exchange for his soul. Once he signed on, the mill would fill up.

The miller hesitated, bargained, and asked for proof.

The Devil, irritated, nonetheless gave in: under Simon's very eyes, two sacks of grain came undone, and poured into the mill. They came out as fine white flour.

The Evil one became less agreeable and grasped the man by his neck. Its eyes were red and its fingers burned. It hissed into Simon's face:

"Do you believe me now, heh, heh? Do you believe me? Sign then!"

The miller, half-suffocated, turned his head to get his breath back. He saw a procession moving toward him. The nuns of the convent across the way had come out, in procession, carrying above them a statue of the Virgin. The scent of incense gradually wafted toward them. The Devil cursed and retreated into the undergrowth.

Reaching the height of the miller, the statue of the Virgin turned its head and looked. In soft maternal tones it uttered:

"Sign, Simon, since you must, but sign in your own way."

The statue them resumed its former stance.

Hardly had the procession disappeared from view than the Devil reappeared:

"So, are you going to sign?"

"I will sign," said the miller in a quavering voice.

Deeply troubled, he signed in his own way. Like all illiterate people he signed with a cross.

The Devil howled. Surprised, vanquished, it fell into a ravine that then closed over.

The wind no longer blew around the hills. On the days when orders were placed and on ordinary days it blew the wings of the mill most willingly.

Tadik-Coz

A certain priest, in Breton called Tadik-Coz, was a master in celebrating the service of the "ofern drantel," the burial mass. No one could do it as he did. Indeed, after his death he could not enjoy for himself the same attention he had accorded to the deceased.

It is recounted that on one occasion he had just celebrated mass for the thirty years' lease of a grave in the north of Brittany. It had taken place in a tiny wind-beaten chapel on the road through the mountain peaks. Shortly after the last prayer the priest took a torch and left for the cliff. Against the rocks stood out silhouettes of demons who had come to attend the ceremony. One of them smiled a toothless smile, and Tadik-Coz saw that he held the soul of the deceased between his clawed fingers.

Other priests would have beat a retreat and left the dead man to his damnation.

But Tadik-Coz defied the gaze of the red-eyed demon and addressed him thus:

"You are haughty and quite happy to hold this poor soul. But he was so miserable and piteous during his life that even hell must seem delightful to him. If you knew the horrors he'd been through! You don't have to hear his groans . . . rather, he utters cries of joy!"

"That is not untrue," said the Devil. "One might say that he is not affected by all the harm we have visited upon him. When I try to upset him, he laughs. When I humiliate him he asks for more. I'd gladly exchange him, but for whom?"

"For me, if you like."

"You?" said the Devil, yellow saliva drooling from his blubbery lips at the thought of what he was going to subject this confounded priest to, for this was the priest who had stolen so many souls from them.

"But on one condition . . . ," said Tadik-Coz.

"What?"

"You other devils are generally thought of as crafty, but I am not dumb either. Let's see whose shrewdness prevails."

"We'll see."

"But let's agree . . . If I lose, my soul is yours; if I win, I keep it . . . but in both cases you set free the one you hold."

"Yes."

Tadik-Coz raised his voice:

"Right, let it go!"

With a pestilential sigh, the Devil opened his claws and the soul became light and escaped, disappearing into the night like smoke.

Tadik-Coz's heart was suffused with a shower of tears. The soul thanked him and was eternally grateful to him.

But the Devil was already approaching him.

"What do you want from me?" asked the priest.

The Devil hesitated. He scratched his pustular skin while Tadik-Coz, imperturbable, stood up straight.

Finally, the Devil sniggered:

"Show me something I have never seen before."

"Is that all?" asked Tadik-Coz. "That at least won't be difficult."

He rummaged in his cassock and produced an apple and a knife. He cut the apple in two and showed the Devil the inside of the fruit.

The Devil looked without understanding and then smiled. He was about to jump on the priest when Tadik-Coz stopped him, brandishing his knife.

"Take a closer look. You must have seen many apple halves. But this one, I tell you, it's the first time you've seen this particular apple."

The Devil stopped dead. He cast a look at the split apple half and his demonic memory must have recognized that the color, size, and pips were not in every respect exactly the same as those of apples he had already seen. He spat on the ground, but had to admit defeat. He disappeared with his posse through a crack in the cliff.

Tadik-Coz looked at the sky where a star was shining, bit into his apple, and continued on his way along the mountain pass.

Entry into the Kingdom

Gospel of Thomas

Jesus saw some infants who were being suckled.

He said to his disciples:

"These infants being suckled are like those who enter the Kingdom."

They said to him:

"If we then become children, shall we enter the Kingdom?"

Jesus said to them:

"When you make the two One,

and when you make the inside like the outside,

the outside like the inside,

the upper as the lower,

when you make the male and female into a single One,

so that the male is not male and the
female is not female, and when you have
eyes in place of an eye,

and a hand in place of a hand,

a foot in place of a foot,

an image in place of an image,

then you shall enter the Kingdom."

The Parable of the Ten Virgins

The Story of the Wise and Foolish Virgins
(Gospel of Matthew)

Then the Kingdom of Heaven will be comparable to ten virgins who, equipped with their lamps, went to meet the bridegroom.

Five of them were foolish and five were wise. The foolish took their lamps but did not think of taking oil, while the wise also took their lamps and filled them with oil. At the gate of the Kingdom the bridegroom made them wait. They all fell asleep.

At midnight a cry rang out: "Here is the bridegroom. Go forth to meet him!" The virgins woke and lit their lamps. The foolish ones found they were without oil, and they said to the wise ones, "Give us some of your oil. You can see that our lamps have gone out."

The others refused:

"If we give you oil, all the lamps will soon go out. Go to a merchant and buy some."

While the foolish virgins went in search of oil, the bridegroom arrived. Those who had been provident entered with him into the wedding banquet and the door closed behind them. When the foolish virgins arrived, they found the door shut.

They knocked and cried:

"Lord, open to us!"

But the bridegroom replied:

"I tell you this: I do not know you. Be watchful, for you know neither the day, nor the hour. Be watchful, for you never know when I might arrive."

Death

An elder of the monastery of Scetis had reached the end of his life. He lay on his deathbed, which was erected in the chapel. The monks surrounding him recited psalms and mourned for him. The old man then opened an eye and let out a guffaw. Despite the cough that had taken hold of him, he wished to open an eye and to burst out laughing once more. The monks hastened to surround him and calm him. The father appeared to be in a daze.

However, the old man opened an eye for a third time and laughed again, softly.

One of the monks approached his ear and asked:

"Why are you laughing? We are all here to weep for you and you laugh!"

The old man whispered in reply:

"The first time I laughed because you are afraid of death; the second time because you aren't ready to die; and the third time because I am giving up all efforts and going toward my final rest."

Then he closed his eyes, smiled, and died.

The Wood Chippings

A man of great moral virtue looked at his cornfield. He was grateful to God for having taken care of his harvests. The corn grew, soft and green, and promised to yield good grain. But then suddenly he noticed a brownish patch in a corner of his field. On closer inspection he saw a pile of charred branches. Someone had made a fire and burnt some ears of corn. Disconsolately, the man gathered up the remaining blackened stalks. Who could have done such a thing? Laborers? No, impossible, as they had been so scrupulous and loyal for years . . . no, it must have been the neighbor. He looked over the hedge and could see his fellow cultivator's field, which was not quite so fine as his own.

"Yes," he said to himself, "he was driven by jealousy to perform this spiteful act. . . .

Well, this is for him!" No sooner had he uttered this than he gathered the charred stalks and hurled them in the neighboring field. As they fell, the wood chippings broke some ears of corn.

A few days later, the pious man gave further thought to his burst of anger. "How could I have given rein to this fit of rage?" he asked himself. "The neighbor may be innocent . . . and I have spoilt his corn and deprived the poor of good bread."

Entirely absorbed in his affliction, he went to see the priest. The priest did not find the misdeed especially serious, but since the pious man was resolved to make amends, he advised him to visit a hermit saint, who lived in the forest.

The hermit solemnly listened to the good man.

"To make atonement for your misdeed and to find peace again, this is what you must do. You must leave in search of a dead branch, separated from the tree, yet capable of sprouting again.

The man accepted this penance joyfully and left right away. He wandered for a long time along country roads. Several years elapsed and the man, now bent double, was relentlessly picking up all the branches at his feet, but he could never find wood that was completely dead.

One day at a bend in the road he was attacked by bandits, one of whom raised his knife at him. The man threw himself at his feet:

"Have pity on me. I have nothing. My death would be of no use to you. I am a poor pilgrim doing penance along the way."

"Penance? So what crime have you committed?

"Did you kill, steal, or abuse women?"

"Good Heavens, no. I threw some burnt stalks on my neighbor's corn."

"What? What a dreadful crime!" sniggered one of the bandits.

"I have been following paths for several years, and for my salvation, I am looking for a dead branch that might grow green again."

Two of the thieves guffawed and poked fun at the poor man, but the third man kept silent.

He thought, "For such a slight mistake, the penance is pretty onerous. What penance will I have? I who have stolen and killed for so long?"

He ordered his companions to spare the man and to leave. He would join them.

Once alone with the pious man, he said to him:

"Take me to your confessor. I too wish to sort myself out with God."

Together they went to see the hermit. The bandit confessed all his crimes with sincere remorse. The hermit set him on his feet again:

"For your misdeeds you are going to look for a river flowing upstream, from low ground to high ground, and whose source is lower than the mouth of the river."

The bandit accepted and left with the pious man. Each one had his penance; one observed the water courses, the other broken branches. But neither found the object of his salvation. The good man thought his heart must have been very hard for God to refuse forgiveness for so long.

Unable to do any more, they returned to the hermit and in tears admitted failure.

The hermit looked at the bandit and saw that his tears were flowing: "Here is the river whose mouth is higher than the source: the tears flow up from the heart toward the eyes. And you, good man," he said to the pious man, "hasn't the sight of this man hardened by his crimes, caused your tears to flow? Is this not the greening of a dead branch?"

The two men threw themselves at the hermit's feet and felt lightened.

The Epileptic Possessed of the Devil

Gospel of Matthew

A young man came up to Jesus and said:
"Lord, take pity on my son: he is
an epileptic and has bad fits, and he keeps
falling about, often into the fire, often into
the water. I brought him to your disciples,
but they could not cure him."

"What an unbelieving and perverse
generation!" said Christ to his disciples.
"How long shall I be with you?"

Christ then turned to the man and said
to him, "Bring your son here to me."

Jesus threatened the Devil and the
Devil left the child, and from that moment
the child was cured.

Afterward, the disciples came to Jesus and asked him privately,

"Why could we not cure him?"

"Your faith is too weak. I tell you this: if you have faith no bigger even than a mustard-seed, you will say to this mountain, "Move from here to there!" and it will move; nothing will prove impossible for you."

Strange Miracle!

The abbot of a monastery had reached such a degree of saintliness that he had acquired certain supernatural powers. However, in order not to change the natural flow of things and not to carry out what God did not wish, he did not want to make use of these powers.

He seldom left his monastery, in order to avoid being assailed by the crowds of lepers, blind men, and other paralytic creatures who lay in wait on his way out.

But one day, his own brother had a son who was born monstrous. His face was turned the wrong way 'round. The disconsolate father pestered his brother, the abbot, in vain. The abbot stole away, not wishing to bless his nephew.

The child grew up with his misfortune. His father was on the alert: every time the monks went out he followed them with his son, in the hope that they would meet the father abbot. Once, for a whole week, the abbot stayed shut up in a chapel he had entered, because the father and his son were keeping watch at the door.

In mid-August, the procession in honor of Holy Mary, Mother of God, took place. On this occasion all the girls of the surrounding villages gathered together, dressed in white gowns, their heads covered by veils. They walked, singing the praises of the Virgin. Seeing the cortège approach, the boy's father had an inspiration. He knew the procession was making its way toward the monastery and that the girls were to be blessed by the monks. Right away he dressed his son as a girl, then smuggled him into the crowd.

When the procession reached the monastery gate where everyone was gathered, the father abbot stepped forward and uttered the holy words over the head of each girl. He was about to kiss a forehead when he noticed the hair showing underneath the hem of the veil. He raised it gingerly, noticed the hair, and understood. He looked around him; everyone was hanging on to his gestures. Unable to escape, he blessed the boy alongside the other girls.

The boy's head tilted up the right way and looked ahead.

The holy monk smiled, satisfied with this miracle that had been forced out of him.

The Mantle of
Christ

O ne day when Jesus was walking
amongst the crowd, a woman tried
to reach him. For twelve years this woman
had suffered blood loss. She had exhausted
her resources and depleted her fortune to pay
for doctors, but her condition worsened. The
blood loss made her feel as though life were
draining from her.

That day, on seeing the son of God,
she said, "If only I could touch his clothes,
I would be saved." Painfully making her
way, and crushed by bodies packed closely
together, she cut a path through the dense
crowd, and managed to reach the hem of
Jesus's mantle. She stretched forward her
hand and touched it with her fingertips.
At that, the source from which the blood

flowed dried up and the woman felt she had been cured.

Jesus was aware that strength had left him. He turned round and asked:

"Who touched my clothes?"

His disciples, astonished, said to him:

"You can see what a crowd surrounds us and you ask who has touched you?"

Jesus surveyed the crowd of people surrounding him.

Then the woman timidly stepped forward, prostrated herself, and told him what had just happened.

Jesus raised her up, smiled at her, and said:

"My daughter. It is your faith that has saved you. Go and be cured of your infirmity."

The Angel
and the Hermit

There was once a hermit who lived isolated in the forest; in the heart of the forest in his hut; in the middle of his hut, close to his hearth. But even though he was cloistered the din of the world reached him. Even there he could not attain peace. He was consumed by a nagging question: "Why? Why are some people rich and others poverty-stricken? Why life? Why war? Why power and why the yoke?"

However much he prayed and placed his faith in God, he suffered and lacked confidence in providence.

God, who was observing his anxiety from his balustrade, decided to intervene. He sent an angel who swooped down just in front of the hermit, who was engaged in digging his vegetable garden.

At that, the holy man dropped his spade and prostrated himself with his face to the ground. The angel, having arrived incandescent, gradually lost his radiance, assuming the aspect of a normal young man. He set the old man back on his feet: "Come, follow me, if you like," he said, "but don't ask any questions."

The hermit followed humbly in the angel's footsteps.

At nightfall they reached a house. At the entrance they were greeted warmly by two good people. After eating they went to sleep in nice warm beds. But just as they were about to leave, the angel stole a golden cup.

The hermit was shocked. But he had promised to say nothing and remained silent. In the evening they reached the edge of a farm. They knocked on the door. The farmer suddenly emerged from the barn, armed with a pitchfork and pursued them, dogs in tow, as far as the road. The angel had just enough the time to throw a bag of gold on a pile of straw.

They lay down, huddled together and shivering in the forest. The hermit became increasingly doubtful. But he said nothing.

Worn out, on the evening of the third day they found another welcoming house where a young couple lived. After supper, the bride prepared a thyme infusion for the old hermit, which revived him after his icy night.

They slept snuggly and deeply.

The next morning they expressed their thanks and set off. But no sooner had they left than the angel hurled a firebrand through the window into the house. In no time the fire had spread and the farm was reduced to a heap of charred beams. Then the angel swiftly took the hermit far away from the village.

When they were at last protected by the clusters of tall trees, and having established that they were not being followed, the hermit turned to the angel and, in the appearance of the redeemer, bellowed:

"What does that mean? Is that what you call that divine providence? It punishes good people and rewards louts. I no longer want your company. I renounce you. I'm leaving. I am going home. God be with you!"

"Wait," said the angel.

The hermit, in a temper, turned around. But he noticed his companion growing gradually radiant.

"You judge when you know nothing. The cup that I stole was not solid gold. The metal was tarnished and would have poisoned them. The purse I left the farmer will enrich him. But soon bandits are going to invade this region and it is this farm that will appear to be the richest, which will be destroyed. As for the good people, they would never have found the treasure buried under their house, if I hadn't burned it down. You judge, yet you know nothing of cause and effect."

Thus spoke the angel, and disappeared.

Attention

Jesus and Saint Peter continued on their way along a stony path. Saint Peter was worn out. He trudged on, head lowered, short of breath, and stumbled at almost every step. From time to time he craned his neck to look at Jesus, who was far ahead and seemed to glide along the cobblestones. He became even wearier. Jesus heard his companion's husky panting and paused. Saint Peter halted, bent double, thrust both fists into his ribcage, and moaned.

Jesus helped him to sit down and said:

"Peter, I will give you a horse if you recite the Lord's Prayer once without allowing yourself to be distracted by anything, even for a moment."

"What a godsend!" said Saint Peter. "A horse! And for something I can do so easily!"

At that, he stood up again and recited the prayer aloud.

Half-way through, however, he paused mid-sentence and asked:

"But my Lord, will this horse be saddled?"

"No," replied Jesus, rising to his feet again. "This horse will have no saddle. What's more, there will be no horse. Let's go!"

Saint Bruno

B rother Bruno was saying his prayers, but he could hear frogs vying with each other by the intensity of their croaking. He tried to concentrate on his crucifix. In an attempt to drown out the racket he recited his prayers aloud, in an increasingly loud voice, but it was useless. The obsessive croaking of the frogs was upsetting his concentration as he was praying. He exclaimed, "Silence! I am praying!"

He was a saint and his orders inspired respect. At once, nature became silent, just as a fire goes out; and complete silence reigned over the marsh. Brother Bruno noted from his window that the toads had stopped croaking, that the herons' beaks were closed, and the flies that remained quite still on the reeds no longer dared to buzz in a wind that had fallen silent.

Contented, he returned to his prayers. But another voice was heard—an inner voice. This small voice said to him: "And what if God derived greater pleasure in the croaking of the frogs than in the chanting of your psalms?"

Shocked, the saint replied, "But what can God find so pleasurable in the croaking of a frog? And what's more, at full volume … Why did God invent noise?"

Saint Bruno returned to his window and allowed nature to resume its course. The insects and frogs filled the silence of the night with their subdued rhythm. Bruno listened to this chant, no longer resisting it, and at once his heart beat in accord with the universe.

From that day on he prayed ceaselessly; his days passed in continuous prayer. He was constantly reminded of God by the croaking of the frogs.

No Lawyer in
Paradise

When Saint Yves de Vérité died, he met on his way to paradise a good many kind sisters who were also going there.

Conversing together, they reached the gates of Saint Peter's at nightfall. The holy doorkeeper was there, before the tall marble porch. He peered over his glasses at the women of the convent of Brunetière, who had died at the same time the day before in the fire that had ravaged their house. Among the nuns' robes, he did not notice those of the lawyer.

But the next day, at dawn, Saint Peter at once saw him among the rosy pink color of the chins of the ladies like a nose in the middle of a face.

"You can't stay here," he said to Saint Yves.

"Why not?"

"First, because you entered by dint of cunning. And second, because there is no seat here for people of your profession."

"I will not be expelled without prior warning!" raged Saint Yves. "I demand that it is drafted by a bailiff."

Saint Peter, most embarrassed by this procedure, searched all the circles of paradise. But however much he went through every floor, going up and down the staircases from the top of the white tower, he could not find a bailiff.

So Saint Yves stayed there because he could not be banished.

Henceforth he is a lawyer in paradise.

Saint Yves
and the Sailor

A sailor who lived in the countryside had to make his way to the port in order to board a steamer. During the journey, a raging hunger gave him stomach cramps and he stopped at the first inn he chanced upon.

He ordered the owner to make a big omelet with a good dozen eggs. She served up the dish, which was spilling over a broad-rimmed platter. The sailor ate with great relish. When it was time to pay the bill came he said to the hostess:

"Listen. I don't have a single cent, but when I return I will pay you without fail."

The woman had to accept this—after all, an omelet once eaten is not to be taken back—yet she felt duped. The years passed, but the man did not return. And the owner did not forget her dozen eggs.

At last, on a fine summer's day, the tide brought back the sailor. The steamboat came back to the port after several years at sea. As soon as he stepped ashore, the man, who was worried about his debt, hurried to find the inn.

"Ah! There you are. It is none too soon!" the hostess said to him.

"Yes. I have spent a long time on the water. But, as you see, I have come back to pay you the sum I owe."

"Yes, I can see that, but today it is dearer! You left three years ago . . . My eggs would have become hens. And twelve hens can have chickens. Some I would have sold, others would have become brood-hens for eggs . . . Just fancy all the money you have made me lose! You owe me several dozen omelets. . . ."

"But you're exaggerating. I only ate twelve eggs and I have come back to pay for them."

"Aren't you going to compensate me? Very well, I will take you to court!"

The sailor left the inn most downcast. He could have had a pleasant stay . . . and now he was going to be reduced to poverty because of an omelet.

A while later the judge let him know that his trial was going to take place, adding that he could, if the sailor so wished, produce a witness.

"What witness could I bring forward?" wondered the sailor. "I don't know anyone here! I shall defend myself single-handedly." He left the barn where he was staying, wandered a little in the countryside, and ended up sitting on a milestone. A man stopped in front of him.

"I can see you're bent forward and that your brow is wrinkled with anxiety. You look most distressed," said the stranger.

The sailor felt greatly alone. The man's tone inspired confidence, so he recounted the matter to him.

"You have come across the right person," replied the other man, laughing loudly. "As a matter of fact I am a lawyer—the lawyer and saint of the Bretons, and I am at your service. I shall be present at your trial and you will not need anyone else. I can throw my weight around," he added, slapping his belly, "so as to tip the scales on the right side. And, above all, trust me!"

Yves winked and left.

Reassured, the sailor awaited his court summons without undue anxiety. On the appointed day he entered the large law court. Instinctively, his shoulders sank when the judge robed in red abruptly indicated his place. The owner of the inn was already there. She did not even deign to look at him.

"Let the plaintiff express herself."

The woman stepped forward and explained that by now her twelve eggs would have had the time to multiply and that without this confounded omelet she would have had a gigantic henhouse.

The sailor was barely listening. He kept turning toward the door. Surely the saint had not forgotten. And yet . . . It was his turn to speak. He would have to defend himself single-handedly. In order to collect his thoughts he took the time to stand up, bow to the court, clear his throat, and ... the door opened.

Saint Yves calmly walked up to them.

"Who are you?" asked the judge.

"I am the sailor's witness," replied Yves.

"You're late."

"But the road to justice is long," retorted Yves.

"What do you mean?" asked the judge.

"I walked past a field of cooked broad beans to see if they had grown."

"Grown? Cooked broad beans?"

"Of course."

"This witness is not in full possession of his faculties," sniggered the owner of the inn.

"Am I really madder than you?" asked Saint Yves turning toward the woman. "Were the dozen eggs that the sailor borrowed from you cooked, or not?"

"Yes, they were ... but ..."

"Your honor, are you suing this man for twelve cooked eggs? Would they really have been able to produce chickens? Next time that madam wishes her eggs to bear fruit, let the chickens let her not serve them as an omelet!"

The incident was closed and the trial settled. The sailor invited Saint Yves to the inn. He accepted readily.

The Eloquent Preacher

The preacher's whole body shook when he preached. He was extraordinarily eloquent, flamboyant like a tower on fire. The faithful gathered in the church listened to him devotedly, moved to tears. But a man in the first row observed the priest with a distant and detached expression.

On the way out of the church the cleric asked him:

"Did you hear the mass?"

"Yes. I am not deaf," answered the man.

"What did you think?"

"I thought the priest was so moving I could have wept."

"So why didn't you weep?"

The man cast a haughty look at him:

"Because I am not from the parish."

The Bad Judge

Jesus said, "There was in a town a judge who did not fear God and who had no respect for anyone. In this same town there lived a widow.

"After having been robbed, she went to see the judge and said to him:

"'Let me have justice against my opponent!'

"But the judge refused even to listen. So the widow returned every day, and then night and day, to complain to him and demand justice.

"In the end he said to himself:

"'Even if I don't fear God and have no respect for anyone, I am going to give justice to this widow, if only to stop her getting on my nerves.'"

And Jesus added, "And would not my Father, who always hears you, not listen to you if you prayed to him relentlessly?"

The Lettuce

A young monk was in the kitchen washing lettuce. A monastic brother entered, and noticing him, called out to him to put him to the test:

"Did you hear the homily this morning?"

"Sure!" said the young monk.

"And could you repeat what the elder said?"

"No, no. I wouldn't really know," said the novice, a little embarrassed.

"Why do you listen to the homily if you can't remember anything?" scolded the brother.

"Well ... it's like the lettuce," replied the novice, "water flows through it and cleans it, but does not remain in the leaves."

Advice

O ne hot afternoon while Father Poemen was in a meeting with his monastic brothers a young monk arrived, looking alarmed, and asked to speak to him. Noticing his anxiety, the abbot invited him into his tent.

"Well?" asked Father Poemen.

The monk lowered his head.

"With my spiritual father my soul is wrongly guided. It grows sad and withers."

Father Poemen had heard of the abbot in question, whose influence was beyond doubt detrimental to the young man. But why," he wondered, did he not manage to take the obvious decision? So the abbot replied to him:

"If you want guidance, stay with him."

The monk, contrite, returned to serve his spiritual father.

For a second time he went back to see Father Poemen and complained:

"My soul is suffocating under his supervision!"

But the abbot made the same answer:

"If you want guidance, stay with him ..."

The young monk thought it was a matter of a hard penance and he continued for another long month to suffer the harmful influence of his spiritual "father."

In the end, exhausted, he went back to see Father Poemen and said to him, his eyes dimmed with tears:

"I can't stand it. I never want to see him again ..."

"So you've had enough of him! That's the spirit!" exclaimed Father Poemen seizing the young monk's hands.

And he added:

"When a man sees that his soul is withering and losing its fervor, why look for advice everywhere? Let him trust what he feels and make a clean break!"

The Visit to
Father Poemen

Having reached an advanced age, Father Poemen withdrew into his tent to commune with himself. A monk from his order informed him that a famous traveler had just arrived. This was a pilgrim of note who had undertaken a long journey through the desert to visit him.

Father Poemen, delighted, received the visitor, who spoke about sacred texts. The old man gradually became gloomy. He ended up cutting short the conversation and saw the man of letters out. The man expressed his astonishment to a nearby monk, who replied to him:

"You conversed about heavenly things, which are too distant for him. You must talk to him about earthly things."

This strange advice gave rise to deep uneasiness in the pilgrim monk. After a night he sought a second discussion.

This time he spoke to the father of his hesitations and doubts, his erring ways. And Father Poemen spread his arms and said:

"That's more like it!"

The Devil's Castle

A peasant, inexperienced and penniless and as worn as a tarnished soup tureen, walked in the fields to glean apples and pears fallen from trees. While he bent down, showing the seat of his breeches, a shadow stretched out on the grass.

"I didn't do anything," was the peasant's automatic excuse.

"I know. But I thought that since you are so poor I might have the seeds you are trying to find for your field."

The destitute man did not have a field, only a house. But he nonetheless followed the lord, who walked his horse. At a bend in the grove he saw in the distance an extraordinarily tall, grand castle. It had a jumble of turrets and sculpted doors; indeed, there was enough decorative sculpture to populate the castle.

The lord dismounted his horse and led the peasant across the halls of blinding splendor. They reached a small room, which was unfurnished but filled to the ceiling with an immense pile of gold coins. Before the splendor of the room the peasant turned toward the lord and gave a start, for the man had the eyes of a bird. His round black pupils were not encircled by white.

"You can see my generosity and compassion," said the lord. "I shall allow you to take whatever you need."

He turned on his heels and left.

The peasant, dazed, looked at the pile of gold as if famished. He did not know where to begin. Just as he was getting ready to fill his pockets, he heard voices in the hall next door. He opened the door quietly and saw two men seated in big armchairs.

"Oh, how happy they are," he exclaimed. "Hey, you! Have you been here the whole time?"

"How happy they are, how happy they are. That's easy to say!" replied one (he was a tailor).

"Yes, aren't they happy," said the second one (he was a baker). "Try to touch them with the end of your stick."

The peasant extended his stick toward them, but as soon as he touched the armchair an immense green flame arose.

So the baker continued:

"If you don't want to come with the rest of us, take only what you need. Just what you need. Otherwise you will come with us."

The peasant closed the door on the two men imprisoned in their armchairs.

He walked toward the pile of gold and closed his eyes in order not to be dazed by the brilliance of the coins. He worked out what he needed in order to buy a small farm and a plot of land. Once he had determined the figure, he opened his eyes and counted out exactly what he needed. He put ten gold coins in his pocket and left the castle. He did not meet the lord and left without turning around.

—

Saint Peter and the Goose Keeper

O ur Lord is beauty itself. Conversely, Saint Peter is rather small and puny. One day this physical difference became blindingly obvious to the Holy Gatekeeper.

The next day, Saint Peter requested an audience and asked God:

"Lord, I'd like you to allow me to take your place, even if only for one hour."

God exclaimed:

"One hour? You've got some nerve! One hour is nothing! Let's have lunch and you will be God all day."

After having eaten a copious meal—for he always ate with relish—God wiped his oracular lips and said to Saint Peter:

"Right, now I am handing the reins over to you. You are God. Do what you wish."

Saint Peter smiled. He had planned everything:

"So, well," he said, "Today is Galambrun's votive festival and I'd like to go."

God was not keen. But having placed Saint Peter on his throne, he had to obey the saint. Nevertheless he added:

"Don't forget that it is you who wants to go there. I'm not particularly keen."

Thereupon, they found themselves dressed as peasants on the road to Galambrun.

As they descended the last hill before entering the town, they met a girl who was tending to her geese. Saint Peter stepped over the ditch and began to whisper sweet nothings into the goose keeper's ear. Emboldened by her comely appearance he pursued his compliments, speaking to the shepherdess of her beauty, kindness, and her sheep. She was not impervious to his charm and observed without displeasure this handsome blue-eyed man whose shining gaze was full of gentleness. So Saint Peter,

his cheeks flushed, suggested to her that she should come with them to the celebration.

"I'd love to, but . . . " said the girl hesitatingly.

"Well, come then!"

"Okay! I'll get dressed up and join you."

"Wait!" said God. "Who's going to tend the geese?"

"The geese?" said she, turning around. "Let God tend them!"

"Did you hear that, Peter?" asked the Lord, "You wanted to be God, so tend the geese. I'm going to the fair with the girl."

Thoughts Focused on God and on a Beautiful Woman

The priest of Saint-Aignan was often seen to be talking to a very attractive woman. As similar incidents occurred the priest was summoned to see the bishop.

The bishop gave him a severe lecture — the sort of lecture that priests make use of between themselves: he reproached the priest for his lax conduct, love of luxury, and the pleasure of the senses, his attachment to earthly things proving his lack of interest in divine things. The bishop advised him to make sure that he observed better the rules of priesthood.

When the bishop at last fell silent, the priest replied:

"I will bow to your demands, my Excellence. But I thought it was better to talk to a beautiful woman, keeping one's thoughts set on God, rather than pray to God thinking of a beautiful woman."

The Priest's Cow

O ne Sunday two peasants went to mass and were greatly impressed by the sermon, in particular the passage where Jesus says:

"Give, and I will reward you a hundred times over." On arriving back at his farm, the peasant was very excited and he feverishly paced up and down the lounge in his clogs. His face suddenly lit up and he said to his wife, "This is what I am going to do. I am going to give the cow to the local priest."

"What, our cow?" asked his wife.

"Yes, our cow. I have thought it over. If we give him the cow, God will reward us a hundred times over."

Now, the village priest was rather greedy. He welcomed with visible satisfaction this peasant who had come to spontaneously offer him his cow.

"If only all my parishioners were like you! Go in peace. God will reward you a hundredfold."

And for his trouble he gave the peasant a hearty slap on the shoulder.

Once the peasant had disappeared, the priest called his caretaker. He told him he had just acquired a new cow and that it should be tied to his own cow. So the caretaker led the peasant's cow all the way to the priest's enclosure. And there he brought out a good strong rope and firmly tied the two cows together with a knot.

However, the peasant's cow didn't recognize her field. She became anxious and restive and didn't allow the other cows to graze in peace. She kicked in all directions and finally went through the fence, pulling in tow the cow belonging to the priest. In the end, after crossing meadows and sown fields, finally she reached her master's farm.

"Well done!" exclaimed the peasant. The priest wasn't lying."

Christ's Debts

S aint Peter was anxious.

Having heard Jesus constantly saying, "That's good. God will repay you, God will repay you," and sometimes even, "God will reward you a hundred times over," he finally thought, "My master is a scatterbrain who gets into debt!"

After a while he even realized that, "If God recompenses you everything he has promised, it would be better to leave before the balance sheet is submitted!"

So he decided to leave his Lord at the earliest opportunity. Jesus, as usual, walked ahead, while Saint Peter slowed down and dawdled. "At the first opportunity," he thought, "I will go across the field and flee all financial worries."

But Jesus suddenly said to him:

"Look, Peter, I think you'll enjoy this . . ."

He grabbed the stem of a flower and gave it a shake. The petals that fluttered down turned into gold coins.

Peter's jaw dropped. Then he crossed himself and walked once more in the footsteps of the Almighty.

Saint Martin and the Two Rascals

Two thieves who met along the road decided to continue together. In fact, they were cast in the same mold. One was as mean-minded as the other was miserly. One was as envious as the other was jealous. But since they feared each other, they respected each other all the more.

After several months of trickery and numerous petty thefts they met the good Saint Martin in a forest. Both crooks recognized right away the man who wrought miracles: "He who brought dead men back to life."

They greeted him and engaged him in conversation, during the course of which they ended up asking the saint if, by any chance, he could perhaps do something for them. The fact was that in reality they were very poor! They were always chasing a means of sustenance. Ah! They were worth no more than dogs, constantly pursued, wretched, and all skin and bone.

"Just think. We don't even eat every day," one of the thieves moaned, while the second one agreed with a hiccup.

Contrite, they then lowered their heads and awaited the answer.

Saint Martin cast a searching look over them and finally approved. He smiled at them and said:

"What the first one asks for, the second one will have twice."

The two thieves exchanged glances. Neither wished to be the first to speak.

If the first says, "I want one hundred cents," the other will have two hundred cents. And if he asks for two hundred cents, the other will have four hundred cents. With their jaws set, neither thief wished to yield, out of pique, to see the other one getting twice as rich.

Finally one of them exclaimed:

"Go on! The saint is waiting for you. Tell him what you want!"

"*You* go on. *You* talk since you're in such a hurry."

Once more the men fell silent and eyed each other. In no time at all they hated each other.

Each thought, "Why does this scoundrel not talk?"

Finally a grin appeared on one of the faces. And the thief uttered:

"I wish to lose an eye."

In a twinkling, the one who spoke first found himself one-eyed, happier than the other who had become blind.

And the good Saint Martin continued on his way.

The Fall

Gospel of Thomas

Jesus said, "If a blind man leads a blind man
They will both fall into a pit."

Straw

Jesus said: "You can see the straw that is
in your brother's eye,

But you do not see the beam in your
own eye.

When you remove the beam from your
own eye,

Then you will see clearly enough to
remove the straw from your brother's eye."

Peace

Jesus said, "If two make peace with each other in the same house, they will say unto the mountain, 'Move!' and it will move."

Rendering unto Caesar

J esus had just told the people two parables
directly aimed at the Pharisees and the
high priests. The latter, deeply upset, were
forever taking their revenge on each other.
Thus, they came in great numbers to the place
where Jesus was speaking to the people so as
to heckle him. The Pharisee who was leading
the group said loudly, "Master, what you teach
is truthful and I quite realize that you do not
consider the station of people. But do tell us.
Is it allowed or not to pay a tax to Caesar?"

Another listened, then in veiled terms
asked: "Do you advise us to rebel against
the Romans or to accept their yoke?"

And Christ replied:

"Hypocrites! Why do you set a trap for
me? Show me the money you have to pay
those taxes."

They showed him a coin on which Caesar's profile was engraved.

"Who do you see there?"

"Caesar."

"So render unto Caesar that which belongs to Caesar, and unto God that which belongs to God."

The Pharisees, surprised and disconcerted, had no reply. They left in silence.

The Quarrel

O ne day two sages who had been medi-
tating for many years suddenly became
aware that they had never quarreled. They
did not know what quarreling was and they
wanted to experience it.

"Right," said one. "I'm going to place a
stone between us."

He selected a big stone.

"And now I say, 'This stone is mine.'"

"Yes," replied the other sage.

"And you say to me, 'No! It's mine.'"

"No, it's mine," repeated the second
sage.

"Oh yes?" said the first. "Well, if it's
yours, take it."

They looked at each other, somewhat
perplexed. One raised his shoulders, the

other spat on the stone, and they gave up
their attempt to know what quarreling was.

One of You Is the Messiah

A hermit was sitting in the back of a cave whose entrance was obstructed by a rocky peak. He was deep in meditation. Suddenly he heard a faint noise and felt called back to the world. On opening his eyes he saw before him, prostrated, the father abbot of a well-known monastery.

"What do you want of me—you who have undertaken this long journey to see me?" asked the hermit.

"I wanted to consult you," replied the father abbot awkwardly. "I beg you. You alone can give me an answer. Tell me: Is it because of our sins that our monastery, once so flourishing, no longer attracts anyone?"

"Because of your sins? No . . . " replied the hermit.

He appeared to fall asleep for a moment. The father abbot, his gaze riveted on the hermit, did not dare stir. There was a long wait; the father abbot could no longer feel his feet or legs; his whole body had gone numb.

At last the hermit opened his eyes. He looked at him and said:

"Recognize that the Messiah has come back and that he is hiding among the monks of your monastery without you knowing."

"What? The Messiah has come back? And we didn't recognize him? But who is he?"

The hermit had already plunged back into his prayer.

The abbot prostrated himself anew and left the cave unobtrusively.

He went back to his companions and apprised them of this incredible news.

"The Messiah is among us, my brothers. He has come back and is hiding right here in our monastery. And we didn't recognize him!"

"But who can it be?" wondered the monks, dumbfounded.

"Brother Cook, Brother Sexton, Brother Treasurer, Brother Prior," enumerated the Brother Gatekeeper.

"Brother Treasurer, that is not possible: he drinks," retorted another monk.

"Why is it impossible? If Jesus has put on human clothing, he has also hidden behind human limits and even within our faults and imperfections so that we do not recognize him. And that explains why he is able to catch us unawares in our faith and charitable feelings for all other creatures."

The monks returned to the monastery and warned forthwith all the brothers who had stayed there: "The Messiah has come back to earth and in the shape of one of us." On learning this incredible news, the monks exchanged glances with renewed attention.

"Who is it? And when will he find it opportune to reveal himself?"

Everyone took great care to behave toward others as if each one could possibly be the Messiah. Naturally the monks stopped judging and criticizing each other; they also ceased to make each others' misdeeds known, feeling compassion and a renewed fervor for their fellow men. Each thought: "And if it were at this moment Christ who was testing me by insulting me." At that very moment all anger subsided, and when faced with the insulting remarks the monk prostrated himself.

The prevailing harmony began to spread beyond the walls. The reputation of the monks' saintliness even reached the most remote regions and became a beacon for men seeking spiritual guidance.

Could the Messiah possibly be amongst them?

The Good Thief

Jesus was upright on his cross. On either side two thieves, crucified with him, were groaning.

The first thief said angrily:

"So, son of Christ, aren't you Christ? If you are save yourself and save us!"

Jesus heard these words but gave no answer.

So the second thief rebuked the first one:

"It is fair if we are crucified and we pay for our actions. But *he* hasn't done anything wrong." He turned toward Christ looking straight at him and said to him in a voice so faint that the air did not stir:

"Jesus. Remember me when you are in your Kingdom."

So Jesus turned toward him and said:

"I tell you, from now on you are with me in the Kingdom."

The Ray of Sunlight

O ne day a shepherd came down from his mountains to take lodging on a farm. Since a very young age he had lived alone with his flock like an uncouth shy child and he knew nothing about Christian life.

On the first Sunday his boss said, "Come to mass!"

"But I don't know what I have to do!" he said, defending himself.

"You will go!" said his master raising his voice. "It's easy. You only need to repeat everything that is said."

The shepherd left for the church in his old shoes. When he entered, the service had already begun and the faithful had reached the moment of the "mea culpa" in the Confiteor. People were groaning all over the place and tapping their foreheads.

The shepherd, astonished, moved along the rows looking left and right. He didn't notice the noise his heels were making on the stone floor.

"Oh, what a pain these old shoes are!" grumbled a man in the crowd. And everyone went on wailing, "Culpa mea, culpa mea." The shepherd found a chair and imitated what he heard, "Culpa mea, what a pain these old shoes are!"

Two of the faithful burst out laughing during their "mea culpa," and the hilarity spread. As soon as someone stopped laughing someone else would be in stitches. The more the faithful tried to curb their guffaws, the more these guffaws surged; peals of laughter that could not be curbed by anything. And when one of them uttered between two hiccups, "Forgive me for laughing, Lord," the whole church guffawed anew.

Surprised and ashamed of laughing in the middle of the Confiteor, people could no longer stop. Some had kneeled down to hide their merry faces on their *prie-dieu.*

Others crossed themselves while laughing. Those who had nearly stopped and who were trying to control their mirth while clawing themselves to the point of drawing blood, suddenly remembered this: "Culpa mea, what a pain these old shoes are!"

The priest, taken aback, gave the shepherd a chastising look, but the shepherd did not understand what was happening.

At Easter his master insisted upon the boy returning to the church in order to confess his sins. The boy objected. He attempted to refuse but the farmer threatened to dismiss him.

So at the end of his working day, without even changing, the shepherd went to the holy place in his clogs. He fixed his attention on the belfry and took a moment to collect himself.

He entered. On this occasion the church was empty. He crossed the nave without seeing anyone but suddenly he caught sight of the priest, who motioned to him from a sort of cupboard.

"Come. Pull the curtain and be seated," he said firmly.

The shepherd entered the recess and found himself in total darkness; once his eyes had adjusted to the dark he noticed behind the wooden latticework the piercing blue eyes of the priest whose gaze was focused on him.

"Do you know your Lord's Prayer?"

"No."

"What do you mean, you wretch? You don't even know the Lord's Prayer? So how do you address God?"

"And you," replied the shepherd brusquely, "do you know how to milk cows, remove burrs from sheep's tails, feed the young, or how to fix clappers in bells?"

"And if you don't say your Lord's Prayer, what do you do in the morning?" scolded the priest

"In the morning," replied the shepherd, "I await the first rays of sunlight. And when the sun appears I say to it: 'Welcome, sun! Your appearance delights me.' And I caper about in the mountain."

"Very good. Well done. That's fine," replied the priest.

And he left it at that, convinced as he was that the shepherd would be too stupid to understand anything. He drew open the curtain abruptly and left.

At that precise moment the sun streamed in through the stained-glass window, casting a long ray of sunlight into the church.

So the priest turned to the shepherd and said:

"Hey. Look! Your friend the sun is here and it has even set up a rail to hang your coat on!"

The shepherd stepped forward, took off his coat, and threw it on the ray.

The coat remained hanging there.

The priest's jaw dropped and he prostrated himself on the ground, with his head in his hands, "Forgive me, Lord, I had not recognized you."

The Lost Sheep

Jesus said, "The shepherd had a hundred ewes in his flock. He led them on the mountain with the tip of his stick. On reaching the hump of the hill, he began to round them up when he noticed that one had gone astray. Without hesitating he left the entire flock, his entire fortune, to go and find the one who had been lost. He knew this hundredth ewe. She was the smallest, the most fragile and sensitive, the most lovable. It was she who knew the path when the others gamboled about and became wildly scattered on the mountain.

"He looked for her, sensing her odor, and searching her tracks. He pursued her along the most forbidding tracks, the most arduous narrowing paths that disappeared into mist, and in sodden fields. For the sake of his lost ewe the shepherd endured thirst, tiredness, hunger, and despair, but nothing would make him give up.

"And he found the hundredth sheep! He found the last sheep, the one who would guide his flock. And the Father in Heaven rejoiced more for this sheep than for the ninety-nine other sheep. On his way back the shepherd did not know whether he would find his flock, but he walked in peace, fulfilled, as one would be after nuptials."

The Holy Grail

Thus begins the story of the quest for the Holy Grail, whose origins go back to the dawn of time and are written in the Medieval Christian Chronicles: King Arthur and his knights were assembled at the Round Table of Camelot. A beautiful lady, mounted on a galloping horse, burst into the hall. She came from afar—indeed her horse was sweating—and asked to see Sir Lancelot. After obtaining the king's consent they left together. The valiant knight was led by the woman through the forest as far as a nunnery. There he met a child, who, despite his young age, was so comely in nature, of such noble stature, and so virile that he agreed to make him a knight. However, the noblewoman refused to let the child leave with Lancelot: the young boy was to come to him when the time was opportune.

Lancelot set off again, brushing past the bracken. This child had such a proud appearance and resembled him so closely!

Several months later, the knights were again assembled at the Round Table. It was soon to be Pentecost.

King Arthur had assembled them so that the quest for the Holy Grail—the holy vase that contains the relics of Christ—could begin. The moment was propitious because the signs came constantly.

First, an inscription had just appeared on the "dangerous seat." This seat, reserved for a pure irreproachable person, had not recognized any of the knights who had come to be seated there, and it had swallowed them up with no hope of return. For years no one had dared take a seat. However, in fiery letters engraved was:

"Four hundred and fifty-four years have passed since the Passion of Jesus Christ; on the day of Pentecost, this seat shall find its master."

A while later a marble statue suddenly emerged in the middle of a lake before the king's castle. At the center of the marble a magnificent sword was planted, set with precious stones, and along the top of the blade the following words could be read:

"No one will take me from here unless it be he at whose side I am to hang. And he will be the best knight in the world."

The whole court, which was gathered around the lake, remained motionless and stared at the inscription. King Arthur ordered Lancelot to move forward and draw the sword, but Lancelot did not stir.

He knew that such an honor was not reserved for him. At the king's order Ywain and Percival tried their hand but neither managed to remove the sword.

They were resigned to accept the fate reserved for those who usurp someone else's seat. On the day of Pentecost the king and all his knights were assembled at the Round Table, each at his place. Suddenly, the doors and windows shut on their own with a great crash. Although the windows were closed, the light did not grow dim.

King Arthur said, "We have seen some pretty strange things here today, and they will definitely continue to surprise us."

Shortly thereafter, they saw an old man appear dressed in a white robe. He was there in front of them, without anyone knowing how he had entered. He held by the hand a knight in silver-gilt armor, swordless and unarmed. The old man led him to the king and introduced him as the best knight in the world, descending directly from Joseph of Arimathea. The king was moved by this. He stood up and led him to the dangerous seat.

Everyone could see the inscription had changed. Now one could read: "This seat belongs to Galahad." And the young knight, taking off his ermine-lined crimson cape, sat in the seat naturally as if it had always been his. The other knights understood at once that this young man had been elected by God.

King Arthur then organized a grand celebration for him and welcomed him. The old man left by pushing the sealed door, which opened wide, and he disappeared with his retinue. No one knew who he was, where he came from, or where he was going back to. Then the king took Galahad outside to the edge of the lake where the gleaming sword had sprung up. Galahad went close to it and with ease drew it from the marble. The king was surprised but Galahad replied, "This sword was intended and destined for me and I have taken it. Didn't you notice that I had no other sword?"

The beautiful woman on the white horse who came from nowhere appeared again in the court. She said resolutely that Lancelot could no longer claim henceforth to be the best of all the knights because another had surpassed him.

Lancelot humbly agreed and the gentlewoman withdrew, shrouded in deep mystery.

Fights and tournaments continued for several days. On each occasion Galahad distinguished himself and emerged victorious.

The Pentecost mass made people reflective. Then came the moment of the banquet. The king, queen, ladies, and knights took their places at set tables. Suddenly thunder was heard—so powerful it made the palace shake. A ray of sunlight penetrated the hall and made it seven times brighter than before. Everyone fell silent, illuminated by the grace of the Holy Spirit. They exchanged surprised glances. Then the main door opened and the Holy Grail appeared. It was covered with a white fabric and floated in the air without any visible bearer. The hall filled instantly with honeyed perfume mingled with all the spices of the earth.

As the Holy Grail passed before the guests, their plates were filled with their favorite dishes. Once they were all served, the Holy Grail disappeared without anyone knowing how.

The aura of divinity was so intoxicating, and left behind it such a powerful nostalgia, that immediately thereafter my Lord Ywain, overwhelmed, enjoined the knights to embark on the quest for the Grail. Everyone was persuaded by his wish, even if it meant death or never returning ...

Sign of the Father

Gospel of Thomas

Jesus said, "If they ask you:
    "'Where are you from?'
"Say to them:
'We have come from the Light,
'From the place where the light came into being of itself
'Established itself
'And appeared in their image.'
"If they ask you, 'Who are you?'
"Reply:
'We are its children, and we are the chosen of the living Father.'
"If they ask you:
'What is the evidence of your Father in you?'
"Tell them:
'It is motion and rest.'"

The Monk
and the Bird

A monk left his monastery to take a short walk. He strolled slowly toward the small wood which ran along the surrounding stone wall. As he reached the first trees the exquisite song of a bird resounded above him. He stopped and listened. The song intensified. Delighted, he stretched out on a bed of grass. He rested his head on the soft mossy bed. The bird's song transported him into pure heaven. It resembled the lapping of a torrent, the voice of a reed. The monk felt the faint music enter him through his ears, seep into his limbs and spirit. He felt his heart bask in the sound of the faint notes. The unadorned music, simple, so simple, passed through him.

The monk listened and no longer thought of anything.

With his eyes closed, he saw, enraptured, the bird chirping on a branch.

Finally, it was time to return. He stood again and followed the stone wall in the other direction. He knocked at the monastery door. The door opened and a monk who was quite unfamiliar to him appeared. He asked him coolly:

"Where are you from?"

"For heaven's sake, my brother, I am from here," the other brother answered, dumbfounded. "Where is Brother Bastien, the one who was in charge of the gate when I was away?"

"I know no Brother Bastien . . ."

"You don't know Brother Bastien? Has he left the monastery? It must be you who has replaced him."

The brother porter, disconcerted, led the monk to the father abbot.

"But," exclaimed the monk, "has Father Anthony left also? Who are you and what is going on?"

The father abbot stared at the monk.

"Father Anthony has been dead for a century! Where on earth are you from?"

Stunned, the monk answered:

"From the undergrowth . . . I just went out for a while, my father. I went out for a short walk . . ."

Photography Credits

Artistic management: Valérie Gautier
Graphic conception: Bernard Pierre
Iconography: Anne Soto
Production: Alix Willaert

Photoengraving: Arts Graphiques du Centre, Saint-Avertin, France
Printing: Mame Imprimeurs, Tours, France
Registration of copyright: March 2005-N°78828 (08062033)